MW01199930

JAPANESE
FOR TRAVELERS
PHRASEBOOK & DICTIONARY

**USEFUL PHRASES, TRAVEL TIPS
& ETIQUETTE GUIDE**

Scott Rutherford
Revised by **William Matsuzaki**

TUTTLE Publishing

Tokyo | Rutland, Vermont | Singapore

Contents

CHAPTER 1
Language Basics   9
The Japanese Language 9
Japanese Sounds 10
Japanese Sentences 12
Verbs and Actions 13
Question Markers 15
Asking a Question 15
The Written Word 17
The Letters of the Japanese
   Alphabet 18

CHAPTER 2
Greetings and Small Talk   21
Politeness and the Group 21
Nine Key Japanese Expressions 22
Hello and Goodbye 25
Meeting for the First Time 26
I'm Sorry and Please Excuse Me 28
Saying Yes and No 29
Saying Please and Thank You 30
Cultural Note 1: Offer of Help 30
Cultural Note 2: Posture 31
Cultural Note 3: Body Contact 31
Invitations 31
Family 33
My ~ 34
Yours/His/Her ~ 34
People 34
Talking about Religion 35
Names in Japanese 36
Talking about Work 36
Home 38
Furnishings 39
School and Education 40
Weather 42

CHAPTER 3
Numbers   45
Basic Numbers 45
Counting Things 46
   Flat Things 47
   Containers 47
   Long & Thin Items 47
   People 47
   Publications 47
   Spheres & Cubes 47
The Clock 48
Amounts of Time 49
The Calendar 50
Counting Money 52
Shopping 52
Buying Something 53
How Much is It? 53

CHAPTER 4
**Arriving and Getting
Around   55**
At a Japanese Airport 56
On The Airplane 57
Immigration 58
Baggage Claim 59
Getting to Tokyo from the
   Airport 59
Arriving, Getting Around, and
   Making Bookings 60
Taking a JR Train 62
Buying a Ticket for Train and
   Subway 63
Stations and Exits 64
Finding the Platform 64
Express Trains vs. Local Trains 65

Changing to Another Line 65
Taking a Bus 65
Using a Bus Ticket Machine 66
Taking a Taxi 67
Walking Around 68
Renting a Bicycle 69
Asking Directions 70
Finding Souvenirs or Particular
    Places 70
Where is It? 71
Japan's Geography 72
Navigating the Streets 73
Location and Direction 75
Decoding an Address 76
How Addresses Are Written 76

CHAPTER 5
Staying at a Hotel   79
Finding a Room 79
Places to Stay 80
Checking In 82
During the Stay 84
Phone, Internet and Wi-Fi 84
Staying at a Ryokan 85
Ryokan Etiquette 87
Hot Spring Bathing 87
Problems at the Hotel 88
Checking Out 89

CHAPTER 6
Eating and Drinking   91
Finding Something to Eat 91
Japanese Food 1: Sushi and
    Sashimi 92
Japanese Food 2: Yakitori 93
Japanese Food 3: Noodles 93
Japanese Food 4: Tonkatsu 93
Western Food 95
Asian Food 95
Convenience Stores 95
Vending Machines 96
Reading a Menu 96
Asking a Server for Help 96
Other Food Options 97
Arriving at a Restaurant 98
On the Table 99
Drinks, Hot and Cold 99
Drinking Alcohol 100
Ordering More 101
Breakfast 101
Dairy Products 102
Eggs 102
Fruit 102
Vegetables 103
Seafood 103
Meat 104
Condiments 104
Problems 105
Miscellaneous Restaurant
    Vocabulary 105
Paying the Bill 105

CHAPTER 7
Telephone, Internet and Social Media   107
Smartphones and Internet 107
Telephone Language 108
Pocket Wi-Fi Routers 108
Useful Apps 108
Messaging to Meet Japanese
    Friends 109

CHAPTER 8
Traveling Around Japan   111
Map of Japan 111
Geographical Landmarks 112
Buying a Shinkansen Bullet Train
    Ticket 112

Japan Rail Pass 113
Buying Tickets for Local Public
    Transport 114
Buying Tickets for Long-Distance
    Trains 114
Ticket Machines for Intercity
    Travel 114
Useful Phrases for Train Travel 114
Reading Japanese Train Terms 116
At the Station 116
Navigating the Station 118
Avoid the Crowds 119
On the Train 119
Exiting the Station 120
Problems and Requests 121
Renting a Car 123
Paying Highway Tolls 124
Taking a Ferry 124

CHAPTER 9
Everyday Life and
Practicalities   127
Changing Money 127
Public Signs and Notices 128
Laundry and Dry Cleaning 129
National Holidays 130
Travel Seasons 130
Cinema and Other Visual
    Entertainment 131
Museums and Concerts 133
Tokyo Attractions 133
Interests and Activities 134
Reading and Bookshops 135
Sports 136
Photography 137

CHAPTER 10
Seeing a Doctor   139
Getting Help 139
Symptoms 140
Examination 141
The Body 143
Physical Injuries 144
Diagnosis 144
Medicines 145
Registering at the Hospital 146
At the Hospital 147

CHAPTER 11
Police and Emergencies   149
Emergencies 149
At the Police Station 150
Lost or Stolen 150
Problems 152

English-Japanese
Dictionary   153

Japanese-English
Dictionary   171

Japan

250 km
100 miles

N

Toyar
Kanazawa

Fukui O

Matsue   Tottori   H   Kyoto   Nago
Osaka
Int'l Airport
Hiroshima   Okayama Himeji   Nara
Int'l Airport   Tsu   Chubu
Hiroshima   **Osaka**   Centrair
Yamaguchi   Takamatsu Kansai Sakai   Int'l Airp
Kitakyushu   Int'l Airport Wakayama
Fukuoka   Matsuyama   *SHIKOKU* Tokushima
Int'l Airport **Fukuoka**   Kochi
Saga
Ariake Saga   ●Oita
Int'l Airport
Nagasaki   **Kumamoto**

KYUSHU ●Miyasaki

Kagoshima ●Kagoshima
Int'l Airport

Language Basics

While there is no quick way to become fluent in Japanese, this book aims to cover some of the most frequently used and essential phrases to help you while you are traveling around Japan. The language is easier to speak than to write—its grammar and syntax is not particularly complex.

Challenges instead lie in the form of trying to decipher written Japanese, which uses hiragana and katakana—two phonetic alphabets—as well as two thousand Chinese characters, or kanji.

An added challenge is the deeply embedded cultural and social codes of the Japanese language, which need years to unravel and understand. Within a group, the ideal form of communication is sparse and ambiguous. Messages are conveyed through verbal fuzziness, context, and implication. This semi-verbal mode of communication is called *ishin denshin*, or "telepathic" communication, which may seem jarringly different from the directness preferred by many Westerners.

This book attempts to help you understand the basics of these cultural and social codes and advise you on how to avoid at least some of the more common faux pas while traveling around this lovely country.

THE JAPANESE LANGUAGE

For many Japanese people, their language is a cocoon that defines the group, the nation, and the race. Recognizing you as a foreigner, the Japanese will often operate on the assumption that you most certainly can't understand their language, even if you speak Japanese well. Some people may talk about you openly in the elevator or in stores, especially outside the major cities. Mothers have been heard telling children in restaurants to "watch how the foreigner eats," especially if the foreigner is using chopsticks. You are, you will learn quickly, a thing of curiosity, especially outside of major cities like Tokyo and Osaka.

On the other hand, being a curiosity can have its advantages. Whatever mistake or gaffe you make, you're an outsider and a foreigner, and your mistakes are generally dismissed on that basis. You're not Japanese, after all.

Here are some terms related to Japanese language and grammar:

WORD	GRAMMAR	DIALECT	HIRAGANA
tango	*bunpō*	*hōgen*	*hiragana*
SENTENCE	MEANING	QUESTION	KATAKANA
bun	*imi*	*shitsumon*	*katakana*
PRONUNCIATION	ACCENT	FOREIGN LANGUAGE	CHINESE CHARACTER
hatsuon	*akusento*	*gaikokugo*	*kanji*
VERTICAL WRITING	HORIZONTAL WRITING	CHARACTER, LETTER	ROMAN LETTERS
tategaki	*yokogaki*	*ji, moji*	*rōmaji*

JAPANESE	ENGLISH	CONVERSATION	WORD, LANGUAGE
Nihongo	*Eigo*	*kaiwa*	*kotoba*

JAPANESE SOUNDS

Japanese sounds must be pronounced with precision, especially the vowels, to be understood by native Japanese speakers.

Vowels

In short, each Japanese **vowel** has a single sound, as in the following words:

a	as in father	*e*	as in egg
i	as in sushi	*o*	as in oat
u	as in rude		

Sometimes Japanese vowels are lengthened. These long vowels are marked in this book with a vertical line called a macron (except *i*, where the double *i* sound is represented as *ii*). For example, the word *sōji*, or "cleaning," is pronounced *so'oji*. It is important to be aware of this nuance of pronunciation, as the length of a vowel can change the meaning of a word completely. For example, *hodō* means "sidewalk," but *hōdō* means "news report."

In regular Japanese conversation, the *i* and *u* sounds are often not heard at all. For example, the name *Matsushita* becomes *Matsush'ta*, and *kusuri*, meaning "medicine," becomes *k'suri*. De-emphasis of *i* and *u* is especially common after the *sh* and *k* sounds.

Consonants

Japanese **consonants** are generally similar to English ones, but there are some important differences:

F   The Japanese ear doesn't distinguish between the English *f* and *h* sounds. (On some maps of Japan rendered into English by Japanese speakers, Mt. Fuji may be written as "Mt. Huji.") The Japanese *f* is not a strong *f* sound, but is halfway between the English *f* and *h*, like an *f* sound in which the upper teeth do not meet the lower lip, and air is forced out through narrowed lips.

G   Always *g*, as in "gate." Often softened into *ng*, as in "sing."

R   The Japanese *r* hovers somewhere between the English *r* and *l*. As with the English *l*, the tongue is placed on the ridge behind the upper teeth, but with a lighter touch.

Like vowels, consonants are sometimes pronounced in two beats. You pronounce the double consonants by holding your breath for one beat right before the double consonant. For example, *katta* would be pronounced, *ka-* (pause)-*ta*. Again, this is a crucial distinction, because a word's meaning can utterly change as the result of just a single doubled sound.

Doubling is especially common for *t*, *p*, and *k*. This book expresses doubled consonants as double letters: *tt*, *pp*, *kk*, etc.

Unlike English, in which every multisyllabic word stresses a particular syllable, Japanese does not stress syllables at all. For instance, although the Japanese word for "banana" is very similar to the English, the pronunciation is considerably different. The Japanese word is pronounced *ba-na-na*, with each *a* sounding like the *a* in "father," each syllable having equal intensity. While stress is not important, however, proper pitch can change the unspoken message and mood.

Japanese language books commonly explain that the subject of a sentence is marked by *wa*, or in certain cases, *ga*. This is not, in fact, always the case. But, for our minimal needs, we'll simplify life by designating *wa-* and *ga-* marked words as subjects. *Wa* and *ga* are called particles and they connect words together, similar to prepositions in English.

Mearii wa (kaerimashita).
Mary (went home).

Note that there is no difference between singular and plural subjects in Japanese. Like much in the language, they are inferred from context.

JAPANESE SENTENCES

Unlike in English, the subject or focus of the sentence in Japanese is often unspoken, implied instead through context. In fact, using the subject sometimes overemphasizes it, flooding it with metaphorical spotlights and exclamation points. This is a pitfall for foreigners learning Japanese, who are accustomed to adding in subjects, as they would normally do in their native language. In the examples below, the subjects "I" and "flower" are left unsaid.

She's Mary.	The flower was pretty.
(Kanojo wa) Mearii desu.	*(Hana wa) Kirei deshita.*
(She) Mary is.	(Flower) Pretty was.

Even though the speaker may not state the subject explicitly, it should be clear; context remedies ambiguity. It is a deeply embedded Japanese cultural and linguistic trait to prefer saying and explaining as little as possible.

Proficiency in Japanese requires substantial patience and intuition for the unsaid. Think of Japanese as a minimalist language, in company with traditional Japanese design and aesthetics.

this	*kore*	I	*watashi*
that	*sore*	we	*watashitachi*
that	*are*	you (singular)	*anata*
this ~	*kono ~*	you (plural)	*anatatachi*
that ~	*sono ~*	he	*kare*
that ~	*ano ~*	she	*kanojo*

Japanese people often prefer to avoid direct and explicit requests. Instead, requests are understood from context and intonation.

Indirectness is a social tool to maintain harmony and avoid direct confrontation. Regardless of the realities of a situation, a request is best phrased and spoken in a way that enables the listener to appear to grant the favor through their own will. Westerners may think it's like a game, this diplomatic finessing of words and meaning, but it works for the Japanese.

As is the case with many languages, perfect and complete sentences are often not normal in conversational Japanese. When offering a cold beer in English, one would not say, "Please have this cold beer." Rather, one might hold out the beer and simply say, "Please." And so in Japanese, too, one can offer something by simply saying *dōzo*. A complete sentence, in fact, would sound stuffy and artificial.

A request usually ends with *kudasai*, roughly translated as "Please":

Please be quiet.	A beer, please.
Shizuka ni shite kudasai.	*Biiru o kudasai.*

On the other hand, if someone offers you something, then you should reply *onegai shimasu*, which can be thought of as "Yes, please."

Would you like some coffee?	Yes, please.
Kōhii wa ikaga desu ka?	*Hai, onegai shimasu.*

To make things simple, stick to these guidelines: (1) When offering something, say *dōzo*; (2) When requesting something, use *kudasai*; and (3) When accepting an offer, use *onegai shimasu*.

VERBS AND ACTIONS

While this book isn't a grammar text, it will be worth your while to understand the basic verb forms used here. Besides, Japanese verbs conjugate consistently and straightforwardly; they're a piece of cake.

The infinitive (basic) form of all verbs ends with *u* (for example, *taberu* to eat; *yomu* to read; *matsu* to wait). Aside from being the "main" form of verbs (the one that you'd look for in a dictionary), this is also the informal form, the one used with family and friends. In more polite language, such as that used with strangers on the street or casual acquaintances, the infinitive verb is changed so that it ends in *-masu* (*tabemasu* to eat; *yomimasu* to read; *machimasu* to wait). Verbs that end with *u* or *-masu* can be used to indicate either the present or the future tense.

Verbs are classified based on their endings and are conjugated into their *-masu* form and other forms accordingly. A simple overview of endings and their conjugations appears overleaf.

VERB *(Non-past, infinitive)*	Ending Type	Polite Non-past	Informal Past	Polite Past
taberu (to eat)	*-eru*	*tabemasu*	*tabeta*	*tabemashita*
dekiru (to do)	*-iru*	*dekimasu*	*dekita*	*dekimashita*
au (to meet)	*-au*	*aimasu*	*atta*	*aimashita*
iku (to go)	*-ku*	*ikimasu*	*itta*	*ikimashita*
hanasu (to speak)	*-su*	*hanashimasu*	*hanashita*	*hanashimashita*
matsu (to wait)	*-tsu*	*machimasu*	*matta*	*machimashita*
asobu (to play)	*-bu*	*asobimasu*	*asonda*	*asobimashita*
yomu (to read)	*-mu*	*yomimasu*	*yonda*	*yomimashita*
suwaru (to sit)	*-ru*	*suwarimasu*	*suwatta*	*suwarimashita*

Let's look at a couple of verbs in use. *Aru* means "to exist," and is used only for inanimate objects.

There is a book.   There was a book.
Hon ga aru. (informal)   *Hon ga atta.* (informal)
Hon ga arimasu. (polite)   *Hon ga arimashita.* (polite)

For animate objects like animals and people, *iru* is used.

There is a person.   There was a person.
Hito ga iru. (informal)   *Hito ga ita.* (informal)
Hito ga imasu. (polite)   *Hito ga imashita.* (polite)

The common word *desu*, which loosely translates as "is," is like a verb, but is technically not translated as "is." The polite past tense of *desu* is *deshita*. *Desu* is used with both animate and inanimate things, and can be remarkably useful.

I am Mary.   It's a desk.
Mearii desu.   *Tsukue desu.*

I am an American.
Amerika-jin desu.

He was a teacher.
Sensei deshita.

QUESTION MARKERS

It is very easy to form sentences in Japanese. In the polite form, you can change a statement to a question by adding a *ka* at the end of the sentence. For example:

It is delicious.
Oishii desu.

Is it delicious?
Oishii desu ka?

I will eat cooked rice.
Gohan o tabemasu.

Will you eat rice (cooked)?
Gohan o tabemasu ka?

A related marker, though not exactly one indicating a question, is *ne*. *Ne* comes after an assertion to soften it and could be thought of as ". . . isn't it?" or ". . . don't you think?" Here is an example of *ne* being used.

It's hot today.
Kyō wa atsui desu.

It's hot today, don't you think?
Kyō wa atsui desu ne.

ASKING A QUESTION

Asking questions in a strange language can be intimidating, given that success is anything but guaranteed. Being approached by foreigners can be equally intimidating for the Japanese. They worry they'll be addressed in English, and expected to reply in kind or that there'll be communication problems, resulting in loss of face.

If asking a question, always precede it by acknowledging your rudeness with *Shitsurei desu ga* or *Sumimasen ga*. *Shitsurei* and *sumimasen* can be used to apologize for just about anything, from addressing a stranger on the street to spilling a drink on your date's lap. ***Shitsurei shimasu*** apologizes for something the speaker is doing while they speak; ***shitsurei shimashita*** apologizes for something already done.

And when all is finished, successful or not, bow your head slightly and say ***Dōmo arigatō gozaimashita***, which means "Thank you very much."

Here are some question words to help you navigate your travels in Japan.

what	***nan/nani***	how far	***dono kurai***
when	***itsu***	how long	***dono kurai***
where	***doko***	how many	***ikutsu***
which	***dochira***	how much	***ikura***
who	***dare***	what time	***nan-ji ni***
why	***naze***		

When traveling, you'll want and need to ask where places and things are. In Japanese, in which politeness is all-important, asking "where" has a normal form, ***doko***, and a polite form (***dochira***, which can also mean "who.")

> ***(Toire wa) Doko desu ka?*** (normal)   Where is the bathroom?
> ***(Toire wa) Dochira desu ka?*** (polite)

As a guest or a special stranger, a foreigner will most likely be questioned with ***dochira***, adding to the novice Japanese speaker's confusion: are they being asked "who," or "where?"

Word order in questions generally, though not always, goes like this: **Subject** (if there is one), **interrogative keyword** ("who," "what," "where," "why," "when"), then **verb**. For instance:

Where is the bathroom?	Who is it?
(Toire wa) Doko desu ka?	***Dare desu ka?***

To make a question with most of these words, you would either point to the object or place on the map and say, for example, ***doko desu ka***, or "where is it?" You can also create a sentence by using the ***wa*** particle you learned previously. For example:

Where is the bathroom?	What is this?
Toire wa doko desu ka?	***Kore wa nan desu ka?***

When is the meeting?	How much is the sushi?
Kaigi wa itsu desu ka?	*Sushi wa ikura desu ka?*

If you are talking with people who you are familiar with, you can ask questions by a rising intonation, just like in English. For example:

When is dinner?	Where is the station?
Ban gohan wa itsu?	*Eki wa doko?*

Naze or "why," is mostly used at the beginning of the sentence, unlike some of the other question words. For example:

Why aren't you going?
Naze ikanai n'desu ka?

THE WRITTEN WORD

As mentioned earlier, written Japanese is where the real difficulty springs up for many people. This complicated system combines four discrete elements:

KANJI: The core of Japan's writing system. Kanji, comprising traditional Chinese characters, came from China in the fourth century A.D., and have been modified greatly over the ensuing centuries. Most kanji have at least two pronunciations each: one or more original Chinese pronunciations, and one or more home-grown Japanese pronunciations. The kanji often gives no indication of the actual pronunciation, so learning the correct pronunciations is often purely by memorization.

HIRAGANA: A phonetic writing system consisting of 46 main characters, used for words or word parts for which there are no kanji. It is also often used in place of difficult kanji that even Japanese adults may not be able to read, or in lieu of simple kanji that children and foreigners might not be able to read.

KATAKANA: A phonetic writing system, also with 46 main characters, used for words of foreign origin, or for emphasizing Japanese ones. Katakana may be thought of as playing a role akin to italics in English.

ROMAJI: Romanized alphabet transcription of Japanese words. In this book, all Japanese words and phrases are given in romaji.

THE LETTERS OF THE JAPANESE ALPHABET

R: Romaji   **H**: Hiragana   **K**: Katakana

R	H	K	R	H	K	R	H	K	R	H	K	R	H	K
a	あ	ア	*i*	い	イ	*u*	う	ウ	*e*	え	エ	*o*	お	オ
ka	か	カ	*ki*	き	キ	*ku*	く	ク	*ke*	け	ケ	*ko*	こ	コ
sa	さ	サ	*shi*	し	シ	*su*	す	ス	*se*	せ	セ	*so*	そ	ソ
ta	た	タ	*chi*	ち	チ	*tsu*	つ	ツ	*te*	て	テ	*to*	と	ト
na	な	ナ	*ni*	に	ニ	*nu*	ぬ	ヌ	*ne*	ね	ネ	*no*	の	ノ
ha	は	ハ	*hi*	ひ	ヒ	*fu*	ふ	フ	*he*	へ	ヘ	*ho*	ほ	ホ
ma	ま	マ	*mi*	み	ミ	*mu*	む	ム	*me*	め	メ	*mo*	も	モ
ya	や	ヤ				*yu*	ゆ	ユ				*yo*	よ	ヨ
ra	ら	ラ	*ri*	り	リ	*ru*	る	ル	*re*	れ	レ	*ro*	ろ	ロ
wa	わ	ワ										*(w)o*	を	ヲ
n	ん	ン												
ga	が	ガ	*gi*	ぎ	ギ	*gu*	ぐ	グ	*ge*	げ	ゲ	*go*	ご	ゴ
za	ざ	ザ	*ji*	じ	ジ	*zu*	ず	ズ	*ze*	ぜ	ゼ	*zo*	ぞ	ゾ
da	だ	ダ	*ji*	ぢ	ヂ	*zu*	づ	ヅ	*de*	で	デ	*do*	ど	ド
ba	ば	バ	*bi*	び	ビ	*bu*	ぶ	ブ	*be*	べ	ベ	*bo*	ぼ	ボ
pa	ぱ	パ	*pi*	ぴ	ピ	*pu*	ぷ	プ	*pe*	ぺ	ペ	*po*	ぽ	ポ

R	H	K	R	H	K	R	H	K
kya	きゃ	キャ	*kyu*	きゅ	キュ	*kyo*	きょ	キョ
sha	しゃ	シャ	*shu*	しゅ	シュ	*sho*	しょ	ショ
cha	ちゃ	チャ	*chu*	ちゅ	チュ	*cho*	ちょ	チョ
nya	にゃ	ニャ	*nyu*	にゅ	ニュ	*nyo*	にょ	ニョ
hya	ひゃ	ヒャ	*hyu*	ひゅ	ヒュ	*hyo*	ひょ	ヒョ
mya	みゃ	ミャ	*myu*	みゅ	ミュ	*myo*	みょ	ミョ
rya	りゃ	リャ	*ryu*	りゅ	リュ	*ryo*	りょ	リョ
gya	ぎゃ	ギャ	*gyu*	ぎゅ	ギュ	*gyo*	ぎょ	ギョ
ja	じゃ	ジャ	*ju*	じゅ	ジュ	*jo*	じょ	ジョ
bya	びゃ	ビャ	*byu*	びゅ	ビュ	*byo*	びょ	ビョ
pya	ぴゃ	ピャ	*pyu*	ぴゅ	ピュ	*pyo*	ぴょ	ピョ

Greetings and Small Talk

A first meeting between Japanese and Western business people can resemble a bad comedy. The Japanese might want to shake hands and practice their English, while the foreigners might want to bow and try their memorized Japanese greetings. Each party wants to please the other; neither party wants to look stupid.

However the initial pleasantries may end up, the foreigners typically want to get down to business right away, while the Japanese want to continue the pleasantries. In Japan, a considerable amount of time is devoted toward small talk and the establishment of trust and confidence. A Japanese businessperson may spend several years developing a relationship with a potential client or partner before settling down to business.

Especially for the Westerner in a hurry, nurturing friendships with Japanese people can be a puzzling experience. The rules are different. One can know a Japanese person for years, and consider that person a good friend, and yet never see the front door of their home.

The Japanese may wear Western clothes, spend years studying English, and eat American fast food, but they are not Westerners. Don't evaluate personal relationships with Japanese people according to Western precepts; there are thinking processes and world views that are simply too different. Just as there are aspects of being Japanese that elude our understanding, the Japanese can sometimes be bewildered by Western behavior.

POLITENESS AND THE GROUP

Fundamental to the Japanese way of life is The Group and one's place within—or outside—it. Where you stand in relation to The Group—family, company, or otherwise—determines the politeness of your speech. This overriding concern with knowing proper place helps explain the (somewhat excessive) frequency of exchanging business cards, or *meishi*, in Japan. A meishi tells a Japanese person all they need to know about their counterpart's status relative to their own and enables them to select the appropriate mode of speech and etiquette. Interpersonal communication in Japan is a constant game of comparing statuses, so everybody can play their proper social role.

It is also important not to put away the business card when you receive it. Make sure you study it, ask questions about the person's role and leave it in front of you to show that you value the other person. The questions you can ask include:

How long have you been with the company?
Nan-nen otsutome desu ka?

Have you been to the United States?
Amerika ni irashita koto wa arimasu ka?

Do you often travel for business?
Yoku shutchō ni ikaremasu ka?

The existence of levels of politeness, from gruff to extremely polite language, makes it dangerously easy for non-Japanese to sound rude or presumptuous by accidentally using inappropriate diction. For example, young men have four different words for the first-person pronoun "I," each conveying different levels of politeness and self-assertion. (From polite to not: ***watakushi***, ***watashi***, ***boku***, ***ore***.) Sex and age of a speaker notwithstanding, the formality of a sentence is determined chiefly by its verb(s). Verbs conjugated with a ***-masu*** ending, of which this book makes extensive use, are always polite and acceptable. Be aware, though, that ***-masu*** is but the tip of the politeness iceberg; other honorific conjugations and constructions abound.

If a Japanese person chooses to bring you into their group—whether for a couple of drinks after a chance encounter on the train, or into a long-term business relationship—then that person's commitment to the relationship is solid. Make no mistake: the Japanese feel very keenly the responsibilities of friendship and relationships with people whom they view as reliable friends or business partners, hence the time taken in nurturing relationships. To reciprocate with a frivolous or flippant attitude is an insult.

NINE KEY JAPANESE EXPRESSIONS

These key expressions will come in handy. While some expressions only hint or suggest at one's intended meaning, leaving much unsaid, others are short and succinct. Note that there are both formal and informal forms; both will be used in conversation.

I understand.	I don't understand.
Wakarimashita.	***Wakarimasen.***
Wakatta. (informal)	***Wakaranai.*** (informal)

That's correct.	That's incorrect.
Sō desu.	***Sō de wa arimasen.***
Sō. (informal)	***Sō ja nai.*** (informal)

It's okay.	It's not okay.
Ii desu.	***Dame desu.***
Ii. (informal)	***Dame da.*** (informal)

I like it.	I don't like it.
Suki desu.	***Suki de wa arimasen.***
Suki da. (informal)	***Suki ja nai.*** (informal)

Is there a/an . . . ?	Is (Name) there/here?
. . . wa arimasu ka?	***(Name)-san wa imasu ka?***

Chotto

A word of diverse use and pragmatic vagueness. ***Chotto*** literally means "a little," but can be used to express a wide variety of meanings, including a small amount of time, a small amount of something, and even regrets. If you want to turn down a request or offer, just saying ***chotto . . .*** and letting it trail off is often enough to make clear that you want or need to decline. (An explanation, however, should soon follow.) In this sense, ***chotto*** can be thought of as similar to the English phrase, "I'm afraid . . ."

Please wait a little.	I'm afraid that's impossible.
Chotto matte kudasai.	***Chotto muri desu ne.***

Hai

A source of great misunderstanding by foreigners, who often think it means an unqualified "yes." It can mean this, but it is also used frequently to acknowledge what someone else has said. In this case, it doesn't mean agreement, merely to confirm that the words have been heard.

Yes, I understand.	Yes.
Hai, wakarimashita.	***Hai.***

Iie

Usually a definitive "no," or used to disagree with what has just been said. Not to be confused with *ē*, which is a casual "yes."

No, not yet.	No, I don't have it.
Iie, mada desu.	*Iie, motte imasen.*

Dōmo

Has a number of meanings, but in most situations that a traveler hears it, *dōmo* is a casual thanks, or a greeting.

Thanks.	Hi!
Dōmo (arigatō).	*Yā! Dōmo.*

Ii

Literally means "good," but like several of the other words described above, is much more versatile than that. It can be used to indicate that something is acceptable or even excellent. On the other hand, it can be used to reject or refuse something, the Japanese equivalent of "It's okay" or "I'm/it's fine."

It's fine weather, isn't it?	Would you like a beer?
Ii tenki desu ne.	*Biiru wa ikaga desu ka?*
Yes, it's okay.	No, thanks, I'm fine.
Ee, ii desu.	*Iie, ii desu.* [negative]

Sō desu ka?

This phrase, which means "Oh, really" is one of the conversation "fillers" known in Japanese as *aizuchi*, grunts and phrases that used to confirm you are listening. (*Hai* and *wakarimashita* often fall into the category of *aizuchi*.) Variations include "*Ā, sō desu ka*" and the more informal "*Sō ka?*"

Sō desu ne.

Another conversational standard in the same league as *Sō desu ka?* If this phrase is said with a rising intonation, the speaker is seeking agreement from the listener. If the pitch drops, then the speaker is probably in agreement with whatever's been said by the other person.

Sore

Usually translated simply as "that." It can refer either to an idea or an object.

That's right.
(Sore wa) sō desu.

I'm against that.
(Sore ni) wa hantai desu.

That's good, isn't it?
(Sore wa) ii desu ne.

That's my wallet.
Sore wa watashi no saifu desu.

That's no good.
(Sore wa) dame desu.

That's true, but I'm afraid . . .
Sore wa sō desu ga...

Kekkō

A word that can be either positive or negative, depending upon context. It can express satisfaction with something, or it can politely decline an offer.

Yes, I'm happy with it.
Hai, kekkō desu.

No, that's okay, thanks.
Iie, kekkō desu.

HELLO AND GOODBYE

As anywhere, greetings in Japan can be either vacuous formalities or sincere inquiries. *Ohayō gozaimasu*, literally meaning "It is early," is an appropriate morning greeting. *Kon'nichiwa*, which may be thought of as simply "hello," is especially appropriate in the afternoon, but can be used at any time, day or night. In the evening, *konbanwa* is used upon greeting, while *o-yasumi nasai* serves as a parting phrase.

When you greet someone, a slight dip of your head can add to your greeting's politeness. Note that among family and friends, however, these standard greetings are too stiff and formal.

Good morning.   *Ohayō gozaimasu.*
Good afternoon.   *Kon'nichiwa.*
Good evening.   *Konbanwa.*

On the telephone, goodbyes among acquaintances and associates are rather brusque by Western standards, especially in the office. It's said that this habit developed in the 1950s and 1960s, when Japanese businessmen traveling overseas cut costs by eliminating telephone chitchat on phone calls to their home offices in Tokyo.

The well known expression **sayōnara** carries a certain amount of finality and sometimes regret to it, and so it is not said among family and friends in everyday situations. Common especially among young women and children is a simple **bai-bai**, similar to English. Another casual and friendly goodbye is **ja, mata**, meaning "see you later." In a more formal setting, you will say **shitsurei shimasu**, which means "Please excuse me."

Good night. *(upon departing)*	*O-yasumi nasai.*
Goodbye. *(leaving early)*	*(Sumimasen ga) o-saki ni shitsurei shimasu.*
I've got to go now.	*Sore de wa soro-soro shitsurei shimasu.*
I've got to get up early, so I must go.	*Asa hayai node, kono hen de shitsurei shimasu.*

MEETING FOR THE FIRST TIME

For the first introduction, the routine is pretty standard:

My name is ~.	(Given name)(Last name) *~ desu.*
This is ~.	*Kochira wa ~-san desu.*
Nice to meet you.	*Hajimemashite, dōzo yoroshiku.*
Nice to meet you too. *(response)*	*Kochira koso dōzo yoroshiku.*
I don't speak Japanese well.	*Amari Nihongo ga hanasemasen.*
I speak a little Japanese.	*Nihongo ga sukoshi hanasemasu.*
Do you speak English?	*Eigo ga hanasemasu ka?*
Do you speak Japanese?	*Nihongo ga hanasemasu ka?*
This way, please.	*Kochira e dōzo.*
After you, please.	*O-saki ni dōzo.*
Please sit down.	*Dōzo o-suwari kudasai.*
Just a moment.	*Chotto matte kudasai.*
Please come in.	*Dōzo o-hairi kudasai.*
When entering a store/house and calling out for attention	*Gomen kudasai.*

Excuse me, are you Mr. /Ms. ~?	*Shitsurei desu ga, ~ -san desu ka?*
Are you *(nationality)*?	*(nationality)* *-jin desu ka?*
I'm *(nationality)*.	*(nationality)* *-jin desu.*
I'm from ~.	*(country)* *kara kimashita.*
Australia	*Ōsutoraria*
Canada	*Kanada*
Great Britain/the United Kingdom	*Igirisu*
France	*Furansu*
Germany	*Doitsu*
Italy	*Itaria*
Malaysia	*Marēshia*
New Zealand	*Nyū Jiirando*
Singapore	*Shingapōru*
United States	*Amerika*

Questions about your life and interests may be no more than idle chatter, but realize also that for the Japanese, small talk is part of gaining trust and establishing relationships. However, be aware that some personal questions may not be appropriate, such as asking about age, house size, or about the stability of someone's company.

May I have your name?	*O-namae wa nan to osshaimasu ka?*
My name is ~.	*~ desu.*
This is my (business) card.	*Meishi desu.*
Where are you from?	*O-kuni wa dochira desu ka?*
Where do you live?	*O-sumai wa dochira desu ka?*
Are you alone?	*Hitori desu ka?*
Are you married?	*Kekkon sarete imasu ka?*
Are you single?	*Dokushin desu ka?*
Where were you born?	*O-umare wa dochira desu ka?*
What year were you born?	*Nan-nen umare desu ka?*
When is your birthday?	*O-tanjōbi wa itsu desu ka?*
Where are you staying?	*Dochira e o-tomari desu ka?*
When did you come to Japan?	*Itsu Nihon ni kimashita ka?*
How long have you been here?	*Dono kurai ni narimasu ka?*
How long will you stay?	*Dono kurai irassharu yotei desu ka?*
I plan to stay ~ days.	*~ nichikan taizai suru yotei desu.*
Is this your first time (in Japan)?	*(Nihon wa) Hajimete desu ka?*
This is my first visit.	*Hajimete desu.*
This is my second visit.	*Nikaime desu.*

27

Do you like Japan?	*Nihon ga suki desu ka?*
Why did you come to Japan?	*Naze Nihon e irashitan'desu ka?*
on business	*shigoto de*
on vacation	*kyūka de*
to study Japanese	*Nihongo o benkyō suru tame ni*
to study Japanese culture	*Nihon no bunka o benkyō suru tame ni*
When are you leaving?	*Go-shuppatsu wa itsu desu ka?*
When are you returning (home) to your country?	*Go-kikoku wa itsu desu ka?*

I'M SORRY AND PLEASE EXCUSE ME

The Japanese are unsurpassed in expressing social apologies. Done correctly, it is a fine art of nuance. Older women, especially, seem to take pleasure in trying to outdo one another in politeness and in offering the most heartfelt apologies, sometimes forgetting the reason behind it in the first place.

Excuse me.	*Sumimasen ga.*
(when prefacing question, request)	
Excuse me.	*Shitsurei shimashita.*
(after being rude or committing a faux pas)	
Excuse me, but I have a question.	*Sumimasen ga shitsumon ga aru n'desu ga.*
I'm sorry, please say that again.	*Sumimasen ga mō ichido itte kudasai.*
I'm sorry/Excuse me.	*Shitsurei desu ga. Sumimasen.*
I'm sorry that I broke it.	*Kowashite shimatte gomen nasai.*
Sorry I can't meet you.	*O-ai dekinakute zan'nen desu.*
Sorry I can't visit you.	*Ukagaenakute sumimasen.*
Sorry I'm late.	*Osoku natte gomen nasai.*
Sorry I'm going to be late.	*Chotto okureru n'desu ga.*
Sorry I don't have time.	*Chotto jikan ga nai n'desu ga.*
Sorry I'm too busy.	*Chotto isogashii n'desu ga.*
Sorry for disturbing you (when you're so busy).	*O-isogashii tokoro ni sumimasen.*
Sorry I can't help you.	*Chotto o-yaku ni tatenai n'desu ga.*
Sorry I couldn't help you.	*O-yaku ni tatenakute sumimasen.*

Sorry I couldn't write to you earlier.	*O-henji ga okurete sumimasen.*
Sorry to hear about that.	*Sore wa zan'nen desu.*
I'm really very sorry.	*Hontō ni mōshiwake arimasen.*
No, it was my fault	*Watashi no hō koso sumimasen.*
(polite response to "I'm really very sorry.")	

SAYING YES AND NO

Saying "no" explicitly is difficult for Japanese people, as directness counters the ideals of maintaining harmony and face. Instead, the Japanese language is studded with well-understood (by the Japanese) cues for indirectly communicating the idea of no. For example, in refusing an invitation to do something later in the day, either socially or professionally, one might reply "*Kyō wa chotto*" meaning "I'm afraid . . ." Message understood. Next subject.

Sorry, but . . . *(no, I can't)*	*Ano chotto.*
Sorry, but I'm busy on ~.	*Sumimasen. ~ wa chotto.*
Sorry, but I already have something to do.	*Ano chotto yōji ga arimasu.*
Sorry, but I won't be able to come.	*Zan'nen desu ga.*
I can't do it today.	*Kyō wa chotto.*
Let's do it some other time.	*Tsugi no kikai ni zehi onegai-shimasu.*
I've got previous plans.	*Sen'yaku ga arimasu node.*
Sorry, I don't know.	*Chotto wakaranai n'desu ga.*
Sorry, I don't have time.	*Chotto jikan ga nai n'desu ga.*
Sorry, I'm too busy.	*Chotto isogashii n'desu ga.*
Sorry, I can't help you.	*Chotto o-yaku ni tatenai n'desu ga.*
Sorry, s/he isn't here now.	*Chotto ima inai n'desu ga.*
No, thanks. *(rejecting food)*	*Mō kekkō desu.*
Not for me, thanks.	*Watashi wa kekkō desu.*
Thanks, but I don't like/need/want ~.	*~ wa kekkō desu.*

SAYING PLEASE AND THANK YOU

In Japanese, there are various forms of "please" depending on the situation. Here is a list of what would be translated to English as "please."

Could you please do this?
Kore, onegai shite mo ii deshō ka?

Please come to the restaurant.
Resutoran ni kite kudasai.

Please go ahead of me.
Hai, dōzo.

Please do me the favor of ~.
Onegai shimasu.

As with apologies, expressing a proper thank-you requires a talent for conveying delicate shades of meaning. For most of us, however, the polite *Dōmo arigatō gozaimashita* is adequate. The shorter *Arigatō gozaimashita* is more casual yet still polite. *Arigatō* or even *dōmo* is very casual yet frequently used among strangers. Again, as with other pleasantries, a slight bow or dip of the head adds to the politeness.

If you're meeting someone whom you've met before, but this time in a formal situation, it's important to reference the previous encounter, and to offer thanks for the help and kindness you received then, even if there wasn't any. A ritual, for sure, but it conveys your recognition of the relationship and appreciation for its continuity.

Thank you very much.	*Arigatō gozaimashita.*
Thank you for your kindness.	*Iro-iro arigatō gozaimashita.*
Thank you for all your help.	*Iro-iro o-sewa ni narimashita.*
Thank you for calling me.	*O-denwa arigatō gozaimashita.*
Thank you for helping me.	*O-tetsudai itadaite arigatō gozaima-shita.*
Thank you for inviting me.	*Go-shōtai arigatō gozaimashita.*
Thank you for the other day.	*Senjitsu wa arigatō gozaimashita.*

CULTURAL NOTE 1: OFFER OF HELP

It's embarrassing when a kind stranger is graciously offering help, and you don't understand a single thing being said, yet you're pretending you do. If you've gotten in over your head in soliciting help, it's difficult to know whether to bolt away or continue the act. If you pick the latter course, play along by offering *aizuchi* (nods, grunts, and other feedback) when the speaker pauses. You may want to say, *Sumimasen*, *shitsurei shimasu*

"Excuse me, I have to leave." Just know that the Japanese feel considerable responsibility when helping someone, which might explain why they sometimes avoid helping strangers at all.

CULTURAL NOTE 2: POSTURE

Certain body language that might not be offensive in another country might be negatively read in Japan, for example, having your hands in your pocket or folding your arms. In Japan, it would be better to keep your arms and hands to your side. When talking to somebody in Japan, place your hands to the side and stand up straight. Additionally, avoid sitting with your legs up or half-crossing your legs with one on top of the other knee. Instead, sit with your feet flat on the floor with your hands on top of your knees.

CULTURAL NOTE 3: BODY CONTACT

Although the Japanese have adapted a great deal to Western people, friendly gestures that involve body contact, such as hugging or reassuringly touching someone's shoulder, are not common between Japanese people, so it might be a good idea to avoid such gestures unless you know that the Japanese person wouldn't mind—perhaps because they have lived abroad.

INVITATIONS

If you're invited to a Japanese home, whether for dinner or a Sunday afternoon visit, definitely accept after a polite amount of hesitation and concern for your intrusion. As a guest, you will be treated royally and enjoy an opportunity to learn much from seeing how the Japanese live. (Such an invitation can also reflect a certain degree of acceptance within a group.)

If, however, you are never invited to a friend's or business associate's home, don't take it personally. The home may just be too small and too cluttered for its owner to feel comfortable having company. They may also worry that you'll compare their compact, no-nonsense dwelling with your Western home, which may seem palatial in comparison. The fact that most Japanese urbanites don't especially like their homes—sometimes just a single room with attached bathroom—is reflected in the many evening hours spent in drinking places, coffee shops and restaurants.

When visiting a home, bring a gift, such as something edible (classy pre-packaged cookies or cakes, for example); going empty-handed is impolite. Contrary to what one may expect, however, food brought as a gift is usually not served during the duration of your visit. If you need to find a gift, the basement floors of any department store will give you an array of choices within any budget.

O-miyage, or souvenirs, are the most common kind of gift—to friends and associates—when returning home from a trip. Department stores and train stations devote considerable space to the selling of *o-miyage*, especially individually wrapped cookies and cakes and local delicacies. In fact, just about anything can be packaged as a gift, whatever the occasion. Department stores, often offer gift boxes of common laundry soaps, and packages of fruits, sweets, and alcohol come packaged together in special gift sets.

Unless a Japanese acquaintance or business associate has a home of substantial size, you probably won't be invited to visit. But should you receive an invitation, it's best to hesitate, suggesting that your presence would be an intrusion. If the invitation persists, then by all means accept.

Would you like to visit my home?	Would you like to have dinner?
Ie e irasshaimasen ka?	*Yūshoku o issho ni ikaga desu ka?*

Isn't it a lot of trouble?	*Go-meiwaku de wa arimasen ka?*
Won't I be disturbing you?	*O-jama de wa arimasen ka?*
Are you sure it's okay if I come?	*Yoroshii n'desu ka?*

It's polite and proper to bring a (wrapped) gift when visiting. Department stores and the larger train stations devote counters to gift purchases (which are also important when returning home from travels). When presenting the gift, diminish the value of the gift with a soft and hesitant voice. It's all part of the humbling ritual and very important.

This is just a little something.	*Tsumaranai mono desu ga.*
This is something small, but I hope you'll enjoy it.	*Tsumaranai mono desu ga mina-san de dōzo.*
I don't know if you'll like it, but here is a small gift.	*O-suki ka dō ka wakarimasen ga dōzo.*
Well, I must be going.	*Sore de wa watashi wa soro-soro.*

I had a great time today.	*Kyō wa hontō ni tanoshikatta desu.*
Thank you for the delicious meal.	*Gochisōsama deshita.*
Thank you for inviting me today.	*Kyō wa o-maneki itadakimashite arigatō gozaimashita.*

FAMILY

In Japan, it is not uncommon for three generations of family to live together. It is a traditional responsibility of the eldest son to look after his parents, therefore some women want to avoid marrying eldest sons. (Even in her own home, the wife must treat her mother-in-law, and visiting sisters-in-law, with the utmost respect, and look after all their needs during their stay.)

That's ~, isn't it?	*Ano kata ga ~-san desu ne.*
Did you meet ~?	*~ o gozonji desu ka?*
Is this ~?	*Kore wa ~ desu ka?*
This is ~. (e.g., in a photo)	*Kore wa ~ desu.*
an acquaintance	*shiriai*
my friend	*tomodachi, yūjin*
a friend of ~'s	*~ no yūjin*
a boyfriend/girlfriend, lover	*koibito*
my family	*kazoku*
my spouse	*haigūsha*
my wife	*tsuma*
my husband	*otto*
my daughter	*musume*
my son	*musuko*
my child/my children	*kodomo*
my mother	*haha*
my father	*chichi*
your family	*go-kazoku*
your/his wife	*okusan*
your/her husband	*go-shujin*
your/her daughter	*musume-san*
your/her son	*musuko-san*
your child/children	*okosan*
your/her parents	*go-ryōshin*
your/her mother	*okāsan*
your/her father	*otōsan*
your/her siblings	*go-kyōdai*

MY ~

RELATIVES *shinseki*	OLDER SISTER *ane*	OLDER BROTHER *ani*	GRANDMOTHER *sobo*
SIBLINGS *kyōdai,* *shimai*	YOUNGER SISTER *imōto*	YOUNGER BROTHER *otōto*	GRANDFATHER *sofu*

YOURS/HIS/HER ~

RELATIVES *go-shinseki*	OLDER SISTER *onēsan*	OLDER BROTHER *oniisan*	GRANDMOTHER *obāsan*
BROTHERS/ SISTERS *go-kyōdai,* *go-shimai*	YOUNGER SISTER *imōto-san*	YOUNGER BROTHER *otōto-san*	GRANDFATHER *ojiisan*

PEOPLE

PEOPLE, PERSON *hito*	BOY *otoko no ko*	ADULT *otona*	ELDERLY PERSON *o-toshiyori*
BABY *akachan*	GIRL *onna no ko*	MAN *otoko no hito*	MIDDLE-AGED PERSON *chūnen mono*
CHILD, CHILDREN *kodomo*	YOUNG PEOPLE *wakamono*	WOMAN *onna no hito*	

Where does ~ live?
~ wa dochira ni osumai desu ka?

How old is ~?
~ wa oikutsu desu ka?

TALKING ABOUT RELIGION

Do you have a religion?	*Nani ka shūkyō o o-mochi desu ka?*
I'm a devout believer.	*Nesshin-na shinja desu.*
I'm not a strong believer.	*Amari nesshin de wa arimasen.*
I believe in ~.	*~ o shinjite imasu.*
atheism	*Mushinron*
agnosticism	*Fukachiron*
Shinto	*Shintō*
Buddhism	*Bukkyō*
Confucianism	*Jukyō*
Islam	*Isuramu-kyō*
Judaism	*Yudaya-kyō*
Christianity	*Kirisuto-kyō*
Do you attend a ~?	*~ e wa ikimasu ka?*
Shinto shrine	*jinja*
Buddhist temple	*o-tera*
mosque	*mosuku*
church	*Kirisuto kyōkai*
synagogue	*Yudaya kyōkai*

RELIGION *shūkyō*	BIBLE *Seisho*	BUDDHA *Hotoke (-sama)*	SHRINE GATE *torii*
BELIEF, FAITH *shinkō*	FAMILY ALTAR *butsudan*	GREAT BUDDHA *Daibutsu*	TO PRAY *inoru*
GOD *Kami (-sama)*	FAMILY ALTAR *(Shinto)* *kami dana*	BUDDHIST PRIEST *Obōsan*	TO BELIEVE *shinjiru*
KORAN *Kōran*	SHINTO PRIEST *Kan'nushi*	BUDDHIST STATUE *butsuzō*	TO BELIEVE IN *(faith)* *shinkō suru*

NAMES IN JAPANESE

Japan has a long tradition of using titles, rather than names, to address people. In contemporary offices, this practice is still prevalent, with the boss addressed by a title, such as **kachō** (section chief) or **shachō** (president). Teachers and doctors (and others one wants to butter up) are called **sensei**.

Long ago in the old imperial court, asking a woman's given name was in fact a marriage proposal (a woman back then was identified with regard to her male patron, whether a father, brother, or simply an aristocrat who had taken her under his wing); if she gave it, she was indicating her willingness to marry. It was only after the beginning of Japan's modern period in 1868 that everyone, regardless of economic or social position, was permitted to have a family name; surnames then became mandatory in 1875. Even before then, however, the government maintained a mandatory family register system, and it is still rigorously maintained today.

Family names commonly have between one and three kanji, or Chinese characters. Most male first names have two kanji characters. Female first names often have one or two syllables plus the suffix **-ko**, meaning "child," formerly reserved for aristocrats. The female name is sometimes in kanji, sometimes a mix of kanji and hiragana, and occasionally all hiragana.

The name and Chinese characters selected by parents for a child are usually chosen with an eye toward aligning their meanings with the future qualities to which the parents aspire for their newborn. After the parents choose the kanji from a government-approved list, the name must be added to the family register, which is maintained by the local municipal office. (A family will often check the register of a prospective son or daughter-in-law to confirm an ethnically clean and honorable background.) Here are some common Japanese surnames.

Hayashi	Kimura	Mori	Satō	Tanaka	Yamaguchi
Itō	Kobayashi	Murakami	Suzuki	Ueda	Yamamoto
Katō	Matsumoto	Nakamura	Takahashi	Watanabe	Yoshida

TALKING ABOUT WORK

What do you do?	*O-shigoto wa nan desu ka?*
Where do you work?	*Dochira ni o-tsutome desu ka?*
When did you join the company?	*Nyūsha wa itsu desu ka?*
Do you like your work?	*O-shigoto wa suki desu ka?*
What would you like to do?	*Nani o shitai n'desu ka?*

I don't work.	*Mushoku desu.*
I'm a/an ~.	*~ desu/o shite imasu.*
accountant	*kaikeishi*
architect	*kenchikuka*
artist	*ātisuto, geijutsuka*
bank employee	*ginkōin*
businessman	*bijinesuman*
clerical worker	*jimuin*
company employee	*kaishain*
consultant	*konsarutanto*
dentist	*shikai, ha-isha*
diplomat	*gaikōkan*
director/executive	*(kaisha) yakuin*
distributor	*ryūtsū gyōsha*
editor	*henshūsha*
engineer	*gishi*
factory worker	*kōin*
farmer	*nōka*
financial businessman	*kin'yū gyōsha*
fisherman	*ryōshi*
foreign trader	*bōeki gyōsha*
government employee	*kōmuin*
househusband	*sengyō shufu*
housewife	*shufu*
journalist	*jānarisuto*
lawyer	*bengoshi*
manufacturer	*seizō gyōsha*
medical doctor	*isha*
musician	*ongakuka*
professor	*daigaku kyōju*
public official	*kōmuin*
secretary	*hisho*
shop owner	*shōten keieisha*
student	*gakusei*
teacher	*kyōshi*
translator	*hon'yakuka*
veterinarian	*jūi*
wholesaler	*oroshiuri gyōsha*
I'm in ~ (business).	*~ o shite imasu.*
agriculture	*nōgyō*

commerce	*shōgyō*
construction	*kensetsugyō*
distribution	*ryūtsū kikō*
finance	*kin'yūgyō*
fisheries	*gyogyō*
industry / manufacturing	*kōgyō / seizōgyō*
the service industry	*sābisugyō*
transport	*unsōgyō*

WORK *shigoto*	COMPANY *kaisha*	INDUSTRY *sangyō*	PART-TIME JOB *arubaito*
OCCUPATION *shokugyō*	FACTORY *kōjō*	SELF-EMPLOYMENT *jieigyō*	RETIREMENT *taishoku*

ESSENTIAL VERBS

to work *hataraku*	to change jobs *tenshoku suru*	to quit *yameru*

HOME

The cost of housing is astronomical in Japan, particularly in the cities. Along with the children's education, a family's primary cash outlay is for its housing. Single people who can't afford to buy or rent often live with their parents until marriage—and often afterwards—or in company-subsidized dormitories.

One pleasure of visiting a Japanese home is seeing some ingenious methods of making the best of tight spaces. Equally interesting is how the Japanese adapt Western things like furniture and ornamentation to suit their own needs and inspirations.

Where is your home?	*O-sumai wa dochira desu ka?*
Is it in the city or suburbs?	*Toshin desu ka soretomo kōgai desu ka?*
city	*toshin*
suburbs	*kōgai*
countryside	*inaka*
What is your home like?	*Don'na o-taku desu ka?*
It's a/an ~.	*~ desu.*
big house	*ōki-na ie*

small house	*chiisa-na ie*
wooden house	*mokuzō*
concrete building	*tekkin*
apartment	*apāto*
condo, apartment building	*manshon*
high-rise building	*kōsō biru*
I live alone.	*Hitori de sunde imasu.*
I live with my ~.	*~ to issho ni sunde imasu.*
friend	*tomodachi*
girl/boyfriend, lover	*koibito*
mother	*haha*
father	*chichi*
wife	*tsuma*
husband	*otto*
relatives	*shinseki*

FURNISHINGS

WESTERN-STYLE ROOM *yōshitsu*	DINING ROOM *shokudō*	LIVING ROOM *ima*	RESTROOM *o-tearai*
BEDROOM *shinshitsu*	KITCHEN *daidokoro*	GARAGE *shako*	SHOWER *shawā*

JAPANESE-STYLE *washitsu*	TATAMI MAT *tatami*	ROOM SIZE (in number of mats) *~jōma*	JAPANESE BATHTUB *o-furo*

HOUSE *ie*	FUTON *futon*	DRAWER *hikidashi*	WALL *kabe*
ROOM *heya*	CARPET, RUG *jūtan*	CUPBOARD *shokki dana*	MIRROR *kagami*
FLOOR PLAN *madori*	TABLE *tēburu*	WINDOW *mado*	SHELF *tana*
YOUR RESIDENCE *o-sumai*	DESK *tsukue*	CURTAIN *kāten*	BOOKSHELF *hon dana*

FURNITURE	CHAIR	DOOR	FRONT ENTRANCE
kagu	*isu*	*doa*	*genkan*
BED	SOFA	KEY	GARDEN, YARD
beddo	*sofā*	*kagi*	*niwa*

SCHOOL AND EDUCATION

For many Japanese children, education is a time devoted to passing standardized and highly competitive tests to gain entrance into the best and most desirable schools, from kindergarten to college, nicknamed "examination hell" by the Japanese. The ultimate goal is entry into one of a select group of universities, which can assure future work in the government or a reputed business. It is well established, if not explicitly acknowledged, that only a very few universities can open doors into elite careers in public service.

Until they enter university, most Japanese students have little spare time, whether for play or developing personal interests. At the end of the regular school day, a second shift starts, either with hours of homework, or at one of the many private "cram schools" called *juku*, where rote memorization translates into big business.

Entrance into university is the start of the easy life. Unlike the years through high school, little out-of-class study is required or even expected at Japanese universities. (Japanese students studying at universities overseas are often initially stunned by how much work there is.)

The school year begins in April, with a six-week summer vacation in July and August, and short vacations over the New Year and at the end of March. Most students go on organized school trips around November, with seemingly half of the country's students ending up in Kyoto. It might be advisable to visit popular tourist spots during the other months of the year instead.

Are you a student?	*Gakusei desu ka?*
Do you go to school?	*Gakkō e itteru n'desu ka?*
Where do you go to school?	*Gakkō wa dochira desu ka?*
When will you graduate?	*Itsu go-sotsugyō desu ka?*
What time does school start?	*Gakkō wa nan-ji kara desu ka?*
What time does school end?	*Gakkō wa nan-ji ni owarimasu ka?*
Do you like school?	*Gakkō wa suki desu ka?*
What are you studying at school?	*Gakkō de nani o benkyō shite iru n'desu ka?*

What subject do you like?	*Suki-na gakka wa nan desu ka?*
What do you teach?	*Nani o oshiete imasu ka?*
What is your field?	*Go-senmon wa nan desu ka?*
I want to study ~.	*~ o benkyō shitai desu.*
anthropology	*jinruigaku*
biology	*seibutsugaku*
chemistry	*kagaku*
economics	*keizaigaku*
engineering	*kōgaku*
environmental science	*kankyō kagaku*
geography	*chirigaku*
geology	*chigaku*
history	*rekishigaku*
law	*hōgaku*
mathematics	*sūgaku*
medicine	*igaku*
pharmacy	*yakugaku*
philosophy	*tetsugaku*
physics	*butsurigaku*
political science	*seijigaku*
psychology	*shinrigaku*
science	*kagaku*
sociology	*shakaigaku*
When is your ~?	*~ wa itsu desu ka?*
summer vacation	*natsu yasumi*
winter vacation	*fuyu yasumi*

SCHOOL	ELEMENTARY SCHOOL	UNIVERSITY	TEACHER, INSTRUCTOR
gakkō	*shōgakkō*	*daigaku*	*sensei*
NURSERY SCHOOL	JUNIOR HIGH SCHOOL	GRADUATE SCHOOL	STUDIES
hoikuen	*chūgakkō*	*daigakuin*	*benkyō, gakumon*
KINDERGARTEN	HIGH SCHOOL	STUDENT	AREA OF STUDY
yōchien	*kōkō, kōtō gakkō*	*gakusei*	*senkō, senmon*

WEATHER

The Japanese dwell on the weather, savoring every small change with unbridled enthusiasm. Newspapers and television trumpet in all earnestness that the rainy season arrived two days later than normal, or that spring's first cherry blossom was sighted. On a slow news day, the weather can be the lead story. Seasonal nuances make perfect small talk—for hours.

There are indeed four seasons in most of Japan. Except to the north in Hokkaido, and the mountains of Honshu, summers are hot and often muggy. Come autumn, typhoon season hits Japan, along with most of the rest of Asia. Most typhoons lose much of their energy over the Philippines and Taiwan before eventually hitting Japan, usually in the south around Kyushu and Shikoku. Nevertheless, one or two typhoons—identified by numbers, not names—usually pack a substantial wallop. Winter is cool in the south, cold in the north, with the western side taking the brunt of Siberian storms carrying moisture from the Sea of Japan. Spring is brief, as is cherry blossom season. A short rainy season from mid-June to mid-July, called *tsuyu*, precedes summer's heat.

When it rains, however light and benign, everyone sprouts an umbrella. If you get caught without one, convenience stores carry cheap disposable ones. In fact, umbrellas are probably one of Japan's biggest bargains. It would be helpful to bring a small umbrella in your bag, especially during the rainy season of June and July. The Japanese will be quite shocked if you walk around without an umbrella, and you'll likely become a conversational topic.

It's a nice day, isn't it?	*Kyō wa ii tenki desu ne.*
The weather's bad, isn't it?	*Kyō wa ainiku no tenki desu ne.*
It's hot today, isn't it?	*Kyō wa atsui desu ne.*
It's cold today, isn't it?	*Kyō wa samui desu ne.*
What is ~ forecast?	*~ tenki yohō wa dō desu ka?*
today's	*kyō no*
tonight's	*kon'ya no*
tomorrow's	*ashita no*

The weather will probably be ~.	There will probably be ~.
Tenki wa ~ deshō.	*Osoraku ~ tonarudeshō.*

WEATHER	FORECAST	AIR TEMPERATURE	LIKELIHOOD OF RAIN
tenki	*tenki yohō*	*kion*	*kōsui kakuritsu*
SEASONS	SUMMER	FALL	WINTER
kisetsu	*natsu*	*aki*	*fuyu*
SPRING	CHERRY BLOSSOMS	FLOWER VIEWING	AUTUMN LEAVES
haru	*sakura*	*hanami*	*kōyō*
HEATED TABLE	HOT	WARM	FINE WEATHER
kotatsu	*atsui*	*atatakai*	*hare*
CLOUDY, CLOUD	COOL	COLD	COMFORTABLE
kumori, kumo	*suzushii*	*samui*	*sugoshiyasui*
MUGGY	WINDY, WIND	UNCOMFORTABLE	SUNSHINE
mushiatsui	*kaze ga tsuyoi, kaze*	*fukai*	*nikkō*
SHOWER	SNOW	RAINBOW	LIGHTNING
ni waka ame	*yuki*	*niji*	*inazuma*
THUNDER	RAINSTORM	SNOWSTORM	FOG, MIST
kaminari	*arashi*	*fubuki*	*kiri*
TYPHOON	RAIN	DOWNPOUR	FOUR SEASONS
taifū	*ame*	*doshaburi*	*shiki*

ESSENTIAL VERBS

to become cloudy *kumoru*	to snow *yuki ga furu*	to be windy *kaze ga fuku*
to clear up *hareru*	to rain *ame ga furu*	to become cold *hieru*

CHAPTER 3
Numbers

Japanese numbers are quite easy to remember. Two areas to note would be 1) that some numbers are pronounced two ways, and 2) 10,000 is a base for numbers following it.

There are two different ways to express numbers in Japanese. First, as in Western languages, there are Arabic numerals: 1, 2, 3, and so on. Numbers can also be written as Chinese characters, which is similar to writing out the word "three" rather than as the numeral 3.

Numbers in Japanese are divided slightly differently than English numbers. Like English, Japanese has units of tens, hundreds, and thousands. From there, however, it goes on to use ten-thousands, hundred-millions, and trillions. The number 20,000 is not expressed as *ni-jū-sen*, or twenty thousand, but as *ni-man*, or two ten-thousands. The Japanese expression for 1,000,000 is *hyaku-man*, or one hundred ten-thousands, rather than a million.

The number four has two pronunciations, *yon* and *shi,* but as *shi* is a homonym for "death," *yon* is more commonly used. Seven also has two pronunciations, *nana* and *shichi,* with *nana* usually taking precedence. Nine also has two pronunciations of *ku* and *kyu.* It will be important to note that you will use the first pronunciation in 4, 7 and 9, as listed below to form 40, 70 and 90. The first pronunciation is often used to combine it with another number such as 40, 70, 90, 400, 7,000 and 9,000.

BASIC NUMBERS

0	*rei, zero*	10	*jū*
1	*ichi*	11	*jū-ichi*
2	*ni*	12	*jū-ni*
3	*san*	14	*jū-yon*
4	*yon, shi*	20	*ni-jū*
5	*go*	21	*ni-jū-ichi*
6	*roku*	22	*ni-jū-ni*
7	*nana, shichi*	23	*ni-jū-san*
8	*hachi*	24	*ni-jū-yon*
9	*kyū, ku*	25	*ni-jū-go*

26	*ni-jū roku*	800	*happyaku*
27	*ni-jū-shichi*	900	*kyū-hyaku*
28	*ni-jū-hachi*	1,000	*sen*
29	*ni-jū-kyū*	2,000	*ni-sen*
30	*san-jū*	3,000	*san-zen*
40	*yon-jū*	4,000	*yon-sen*
50	*go-jū*	5,000	*go-sen*
60	*roku-jū*	6,000	*roku-sen*
70	*nana-jū*	7,000	*nana-sen*
80	*hachi-jū*	8,000	*hassen*
90	*kyū-jū*	9,000	*kyū-sen*
100	*hyaku*	10,000	*ichi-man*
200	*ni-hyaku*	100,000	*jū-man*
300	*san-byaku*	1,000,000	*hyaku-man*

LENGTH	WEIGHT	AREA, WIDTH	SPEED
nagasa	*omosa*	*hirosa*	*hayasa*
HEIGHT	WEIGHT *(people only)*	VOLUME	DEPTH
takasa	*taijū*	*taiseki*	*fukasa*

COUNTING THINGS

Counting things in Japanese is more complicated than doing so in English. Rather than just saying a number and then an object, in Japanese you must also add a suffix called a "counter." To say "two books," (book is "*hon*" in Japanese), you wouldn't just say *ni hon.* You would add the suffix *-satsu*—the counter for books—and say *hon ni-satsu.*

There are many different counters for different types of objects. Some counters are applied to objects of certain shapes. The suffix *-mai* is a counter that can be used for any flat object, be it a mirror or a pizza. *Kagami go-mai* means "five mirrors," while *pizza ichi-mai* means "one pizza." Other counters are object-specific. Objects that have their own counters include guns (*-chō*) and even chopsticks (*-zen*).

Being able to use appropriate counters is a matter of sheer memory power. Fortunately, there is a simpler (somewhat, anyway) system for counting fewer than ten objects other than people. Furthermore, since Japanese people are also aware of how complicated this system is, they will not be surprised if this is a challenge for you.

1	*hitotsu*	4	*yottsu*	7	*nanatsu*	9	*kokonotsu*
2	*futatsu*	5	*itsutsu*	8	*yattsu*	10	*tō*
3	*mittsu*	6	*muttsu*				

FLAT THINGS

-MAI
paper, cloth, pizza, window glass

1	*ichi-mai*	6	*roku-mai*
2	*ni-mai*	7	*nana-mai*
3	*san-mai*	8	*hachi-mai*
4	*yon-mai*	9	*kyū-mai*
5	*go-mai*	10	*jū-mai*

CONTAINERS

-HAI, -BAI, -PAI
cups, bowls, glasses

1	*ippai*	6	*roppai*
2	*ni-hai*	7	*nana-hai*
3	*san-bai*	8	*hachi-hai*
4	*yon-hai*	9	*kyū-hai*
5	*go-hai*	10	*jippai*

LONG & THIN ITEMS

-HON, -BON, -PON
pencils, pens, bottles

1	*ippon*	6	*roppon*
2	*ni-hon*	7	*nana-hon*
3	*san-bon*	8	*happon*
4	*yon-hon*	9	*kyū-hon*
5	*go-hon*	10	*jippon*

PEOPLE

-NIN
people

1	*hitori*	6	*roku-nin*
2	*futari*	7	*nana-nin*
3	*san-nin*	8	*hachi-nin*
4	*yo-nin*	9	*kyū-nin*
5	*go-nin*	10	*jū-nin*

PUBLICATIONS

-SATSU
magazines, books

1	*issatsu*	6	*roku-satsu*
2	*ni-satsu*	7	*nana-satsu*
3	*san-satsu*	8	*hassatsu*
4	*yon-satsu*	9	*kyū-satsu*
5	*go-satsu*	10	*jussatsu*

SPHERES & CUBES

-KO
small round things, boxes

1	*ikko*	6	*rokko*
2	*ni-ko*	7	*nana-ko*
3	*san-ko*	8	*hachi-ko*
4	*yon-ko*	9	*kyū-ko*
5	*go-ko*	10	*jukko*

ESSENTIAL VERBS

to count	to calculate	to add up
kazoeru	*keisan suru*	*gōkei suru*

THE CLOCK

When is it/that?	*(Sore wa) Itsu desu ka?*
When was it/that?	*(Sore wa) Itsu deshita ka?*
What time is it?	*Ima nan-ji desu ka?*
It's ~.	*~ desu*
1 o'clock	*ichi-ji*
2 o'clock	*ni-ji*
3 o'clock	*san-ji*
4 o'clock	*yo-ji*
5 o'clock	*go-ji*
6 o'clock	*roku-ji*
7 o'clock	*shichi-ji*
8 o'clock	*hachi-ji*
9 o'clock	*ku-ji*
10 o'clock	*jū-ji*
11 o'clock	*jū-ichi-ji*
12 o'clock	*jū-ni-ji*
What time is it from?	*Nan-ji kara desu ka?*
It's from ~.	*~ kara desu.*
What time is it until?	*Nan-ji made desu ka?*
It's until ~.	*~ made desu.*
at 1 o'clock	*ichi-ji ni*
at about 1 o'clock	*ichi-ji goro ni*
at 1 o'clock sharp	*ichi-ji chōdo ni*
~ a.m.	*gozen ~*
~ p.m.	*gogo ~*
half past ~	*~ han*
before ~	*~ mae*
after ~	*~ sugi*
until ~	*~ made*
by ~	*~ made ni*

AMOUNTS OF TIME

| How long will/does it take? | *Dono kurai kakarimasu ka?* |
| How long does it take? | |

How long will/does it take?   *Dono kurai kakarimasu ka?*
It takes/will take ~.   *~ kakarimasu.*
How long did it take?   *Dono kurai kakarimashita ka?*
It took ~.   *~ kakarimashita.*
When will it be ready?   *Itsu dekimasu ka?*

MINUTE	*funkan*	HOUR	*jikan*
1 minute	*ippunkan*	1 hour	*ichi jikan*
2 minutes	*ni-funkan*	2 hours	*ni jikan*
3 minutes	*san-punkan*	6 hours	*roku jikan*
4 minutes	*yon-punkan*	12 hours	*jū ni jikan*
5 minutes	*go-funkan*	every ~	*~ goto*
6 minutes	*roppunkan*	exactly ~	*~ chōdo*
7 minutes	*nana-funkan*	about ~	*~ yaku*
8 minutes	*happunkan*	within ~	*~ inai*
9 minutes	*kyū-funkan*	over ~	*~ ijō*
10 minutes	*jippunkan*	~ ago	*~ mae*
30 minutes	*san jippunkan*	~ later	*~ go*
several minutes	*sūfunkan*	several hours	*sūjikan*

Please note that if you keep the *kan* after the minutes, you can use the above to help express time. For example:

> 1:31 p.m. would be *gogo ichiji sanju ippun*
> 5:45 a.m. would be *gozen goji yonju gofun*
> 1 hour would be *ichijikan*

DAY	*nichikan/-ka-kan*	WEEK	*shūkan*
1 day	*ichi nichi*	1 week	*isshūkan*
2 days	*futsuka-kan*	2 weeks	*ni-shūkan*
3 days	*mikka-kan*	3 weeks	*san-shūkan*
several days	*sūjitsu-kan*	several weeks	*sūshūkan*

MONTH	*-ka getsukan*	YEAR	*nenkan*
1 month	*ikka getsukan*	half a year	*hantoshikan*
2 months	*ni-ka getsukan*	1 year	*ichi-nenkan*
3 months	*san-ka getsukan*	2 years	*ni-nenkan*
several months	*sū-ka getsukan*	several years	*sū-nenkan*

49

THE CALENDAR

When is it/that?	*(Sore wa) Itsu desu ka?*
When was it/that?	*(Sore wa) Itsu deshita ka?*
What day is it?	*Nan-yōbi desu ka?*
It's ~.	*~ desu.*
Monday	*Getsu-yōbi*
Tuesday	*Ka-yōbi*
Wednesday	*Sui-yōbi*
Thursday	*Moku-yōbi*
Friday	*Kin-yōbi*
Saturday	*Do-yōbi*
Sunday	*Nichi-yōbi*
What month is it?	*Nan-gatsu desu ka?*
It's ~.	*~ desu.*
January	*Ichi-gatsu*
February	*Ni-gatsu*
March	*San-gatsu*
April	*Shi-gatsu*
May	*Go-gatsu*
June	*Roku-gatsu*
July	*Shichi-gatsu*
August	*Hachi-gatsu*
September	*Ku-gatsu*
October	*Jū-gatsu*
November	*Jūichi-gatsu*
December	*Jūni-gatsu*
daytime	*hiruma*
weekday	*heijitsu*
every day	*mainichi*
every other day	*ichi nichi oki*
half a day	*han'nichi*
morning	*asa*
a.m.	*gozen*
noon	*hiru*
afternoon, p.m.	*gogo*
evening, late afternoon	*yūgata*
evening, night	*yoru*

middle of the night	*mayonaka*
midnight	*yonaka*
last Monday	*senshū no Getsu-yōbi*
this Monday	*konshū no Getsu-yōbi*
next Monday	*raishū no Getsu-yōbi*
day before yesterday	*ototoi*
yesterday	*kinō*
today	*kyō*
this morning	*kesa*
tonight/this evening	*kon'ya*
tonight/this evening	*konban*
tomorrow	*ashita*
tomorrow morning	*ashita no asa*
day after tomorrow	*asatte*

WEEK	*shū*	next week	*raishū*
every week	*maishū*	week after next	*saraishū*
week before last	*sensenshū*	every other week	*isshūkan oki*
last week	*senshū*	weekday	*heijitsu*
this week	*konshū*	weekend	*shūmatsu*

MONTH	*tsuki, gatsu, getsu*
every month	*maitsuki*
every other month	*ikkagetsu oki*
first third of a month	*jōjun*
middle third of a month	*chūjun*
last third of a month	*gejun*
end of the month	*getsumatsu*
two months ago	*sensengetsu*
last month	*sengetsu*
this month	*kongetsu*
next month	*raigetsu*
month after next	*saraigetsu*
middle of next month	*raigetsu no naka goro*
end of this month	*kongetsu no sue, kongetsumatsu*

YEAR	*toshi*	half a year	*hantoshi*
what year	*nan-nen*	year before last	*ototoshi, issaku-nen*
every year	*maitoshi*	last year	*kyonen*
every other year	*ichi-nen oki*	this year	*kotoshi*

next year	*rainen*	leap year	*urū doshi*
year after next	*sarainen*	end of the year	*nenmatsu*
present times	*gendai*	future	*mirai*
present, now	*genzai*	future, days yet to come	*shōrai*
these days, recently	*saikin*		

COUNTING MONEY

Japanese currency uses both coins and paper money. The coins are as follows: 1, 5, 10, 50, 100, and 500. The 5 and 50 *yen* (pronounced *en* in Japanese and denoted by ¥) coins have a hole in the middle which make them very easy to distinguish. The paper money is as follows: 1,000, 2,000 (not seen too often), 5,000, and 10,000.

Japanese still often use cash to purchase their goods, although debit and credit cards are widely accepted. In many places you will be able to pay with your Welcome Suica or Pasmo Passport card (see page 63). Contactless payments such as Apple Pay or scanning barcodes or QR codes with smartphones are becoming more and more popular. If you are traveling to Japan and would like to withdraw money to get cash, you can withdraw cash at most Japanese ATMs, provided you have authorized your card for overseas use with your home bank. Most convenience stores have ATMs, including 7-Eleven, Lawson and Family Mart, and they are open twenty-four hours.

In Japan, haggling is rare, if not nonexistent, perhaps only possible at market stalls or small shops. The price that is written on the item also includes the tax, which makes it convenient to pay. Additionally, tips are not left at restaurants or given at hotels.

It is also important to note that Japanese try to keep their money clean and as crisp as possible. Try not to wrinkle it or fold it excessively.

SHOPPING

Japan is a great place for shopping. You will often find big department stores with ten or more floors that sells everything you can imagine. There are clerks scattered abundantly throughout the store to assist you. The bottom two floors (usually the two basement floors) of a department store are usually filled with food. The clerks will wrap your merchandise neatly so that you can take them back to your country or enjoy it yourself.

The bigger shopping centers are usually part of the major train stations which make it convenient for you to quickly get off the train and find the department stores you desire. Japanese train stations are usually massive, but there are plenty of signs and station staff to help you navigate your way to where you would like to go.

BUYING SOMETHING

It is quite easy to purchase things in Japan. There are usually plenty of displays and staff to help you choose the product and help you pay for it. Once you find something that you would like to purchase, just bring the item to the cash register. Most of the bigger stores have signs written in both English and Japanese. If paying by cash or card, you usually put your money or your card on a small tray. The clerk will also give you the change either on the tray or on your hand. Most clerks will count the money for you to double check that they have given you the correct amount.

In Japan, customers are treated very kindly. Staff often say *irasshaimase*, or welcome. They will also thank you multiple times after your purchase. As the customer, you should not thank them as that will make them uncomfortable and is not part of the culture. You can either bow slightly or continue your way out of the store.

You can also find information on duty free purchases at the bigger stores. Make sure that you bring your passport with you to take advantage of this.

HOW MUCH IS IT?

If you need to ask the price of an item, you can simply point to it and say, *Ikura desu ka?* Many clerks also carry a calculator, pen, and paper with them so that if you don't understand the price they are saying, they can simply write it down for you or show you the figure on the calculator. Most Japanese people know some English to help you through the process of purchasing things, especially in bigger cities and in bigger stores.

Arriving and Getting Around

Travel in Japan is expensive. But travel expenses can be tempered by staying at hostels, using rail passes, taking local buses, and eating *onigiri* rice balls or cheap bowls of noodles. Especially in bigger cities, you can find great deals at restaurants because of the volume of places in one area. Japan also has many restaurants with inexpensive set menus, especially for breakfast and lunch, many of which can be found near train stations.

You should carry cash and your debit and credit cards to get around Japan. A Welcome Suica card or Pasmo Passport card is also very useful (see page 63). Although it is a safe country, there are always incidences of pickpocketing, especially in more crowded areas.

Organized tourism in Japan is highly developed and ubiquitous. But with a little planning and research, you should be able to travel around the country on your own, especially if you are interested in seeing the major cities.

Wise travelers try to avoid travel during Japan's three prime holiday seasons: New Year's (25 December to 10 January), Golden Week (28 April to 6 May), and O-bon (roughly 21 July to 30 August). Stay put and don't come to Japan during those weeks. Downtown Tokyo can be pleasant then though, as it's nearly empty. Although there might be festivities during these holidays such as fireworks during O-bon, flights are usually the most expensive and some stores may be closed.

There are a number of airports that you can use to fly into Japan. In the Kansai area, the Kansai International Airport serves many carriers. If you are traveling to Tokyo, there are two airports that you can fly into: Haneda and Narita. There are some flights from the US that now fly into Haneda in the morning which effectively gives you an extra day to spend in Japan. Haneda is also much closer to central Tokyo than Narita.

Immigration and customs procedures can be carried out online before you arrive using the website Visit Japan Web (services.digital.go.jp/en/visit-japan-web/). For visitors unable to carry out immigration procedures online, a paper immigration card can be filled out manually. Baggage comes out very quickly. At Japanese airports, you should be able to find English-speaking staff to help you if you have any difficulties.

AT A JAPANESE AIRPORT

I want to check in.	*Chekku-in shitai n'desu ga.*
I want to make a reservation.	*Yoyaku o shitai n'desu ga.*
I've made a reservation.	*Yoyaku shimashita.*
The reservation was confirmed in ~.	*Yoyaku wa ~ de kakunin shite arimasu.*
I'd like to reconfirm my reservation.	*Yoyaku no saikakunin o shitai n'desu ga.*
I want to change my flight.	*Furaito o henkō shitai n'desu ga.*
I'd like to ~ my reservation.	*Yoyaku o ~ shitai n'desu ga.*
confirm	*kakunin*
cancel	*kyanseru*
change	*henkō*
Cancel this reservation, please.	*Kono yoyaku o kyanseru shite kudasai.*
I just missed my flight.	*Hikōki ni noriokuremashita.*
I missed my connecting flight. Help.	*Noritsugi ni okuremashita. Tasukete kudasai.*
Has the counter closed?	*Kauntā wa mō shimarimashita ka?*
Is there somewhere I can stay for the night (free of charge)?	*Muryō de tomareru tokoro wa arimasu ka?*
The plane was delayed.	*Hikōki ga okuremashita.*
How do I check in?	*Dono yo ni chekku-in dekimasu ka?*
When is the next available flight to ~?	*Tsugi no ~ yuki no bin wa nan-ji desu ka?*
Do you have any seats?	*Seki wa arimasu ka?*
Is there a /an ~ flight?	*~ no bin wa arimasu ka?*
morning	*gozen*
afternoon	*gogo*
evening	*yoru*
Is there an earlier flight?	*Sore yori hayai bin ga arimasu ka?*
Is there a later flight?	*Sore yori osoi bin ga arimasu ka?*

CHECK-IN	DESTINATION	DEPARTURE	ARRIVAL	TIMETABLE
chekku-in	*yukisaki*	*shuppatsu*	*tōchaku*	*jikokuhyō*

How much is it?	*Ikura desu ka?*
How much is a one-way ticket to ~?	*~ made katamichi ikura desu ka?*
How much is a round trip ticket to ~?	*~ made ōfuku ikura desu ka?*

One ticket to ~, please.	*~ yuki no kippu o ichi-mai kudasai.*
Round trip to ~, please.	*~ made ōfuku kippu kudasai.*
One-way to ~, please.	*~ made katamichi kippu kudasai.*
Window seat, please.	*Madogawa no seki ni shite kudasai.*
Aisle seat, please.	*Tsūrogawa no seki ni shite kudasai.*
No smoking seat, please.	*Kin'enseki ni shite kudasai.*
This is my baggage.	*Kore ga watashi no nimotsu desu.*
hand luggage	*te-nimotsu*
I'd like to check this.	*Kore o azuketai n'desu ga.*
This one is fragile.	*Waremono ga haitte imasu.*
How much is the excess baggage charge?	*Chōka ryōkin wa ikura desu ka?*
When is the boarding time?	*Tōjō kaishi wa nan-ji desu ka?*
Will this flight leave on time?	*Kono bin wa yotei dōri demasu ka?*
How long is the delay?	*Dono kurai okuremasu ka?*

AIRPORT *kūkō*	DOMESTIC FLIGHT *kokunaisen*	AIRLINE TICKET *kōkūken*	OPEN SEATING *jiyūseki*
AIRLINE COMPANY *kōkū gaisha*	FLIGHT NUMBER *binmei*	ECONOMY CLASS *ekonomii kurasu*	EXCESS BAG CHARGE *chōka ryōkin*
AIRPLANE *hikōki*	FARE *unchin*	FIRST CLASS *fāsuto kurasu*	BAGGAGE *te-nimotsu*
INTERNATIONAL FLIGHT *kokusaisen*	GATE *gēto*	NO SMOKING *kin'en*	SUITCASE *sūtsukēsu*

ON THE AIRPLANE

Where is this seat?	*Kono seki wa dono hen desu ka?*
May I sit here?	*Kono seki ni suwatte ii desu ka?*
May I get through?	*Chotto tōshite kudasai.*

OCCUPIED *shiyōchū*	VACANT *aki*	SEAT NUMBER *zaseki bangō*	BOARDING PASS *tōjōken*	DRINK *nomimono*

IMMIGRATION

After you collect your luggage, you will pass through immigration and then customs. There is a separate immigration queue for foreigners. If you have carried out immigration procedures online using Visit Japan Web (see page 55) you will be issued with a QR code for swift and easy progress through immigration and customs. If you have filled in a paper form, these processes will take more time. As of spring 2024, most nationalities can stay for up to ninety days in Japan without a visa. The website of the Japanese Ministry of Foreign Affairs gives up-to-date visa requirements (mofa.go.jp/j_info/visit/visa/short/novisa.html).

It is possible that customs staff may ask you questions in basic English, and may also show you pictures of what they are talking about: drugs and guns. Don't even joke about them. Handguns and drugs are illegal, and punishments are severe.

I'll stay at ~ hotel.	*~ hoteru de tomarimasu.*
These are all my personal belongings.	*Zenbu mi no mawarihin desu.*
This is a gift for a friend.	*Kore wa yūjin e no miyagehin desu.*

PASSPORT CONTROL *nyūkoku shinsa*	RESIDENT *(of Japan)* *kyojūsha*	NATIONALITY *kokuseki*	SINGLE *dokushin*
CUSTOMS *zeikan*	NONRESIDENT *hi-kyojūsha*	ADDRESS IN JAPAN *kokunai renrakusaki*	OCCUPATION *shokugyō*
PASSPORT *pasupōto*	NAME *namae*	PERMANENT ADDRESS *honseki*	PURPOSE OF VISIT *ryokō mokuteki*
VISA *sashō, biza*	FIRST NAME *namae*	DATE OF BIRTH *seinen-gappi*	MARRIED *kikon*
FOREIGNER *gaikoku-jin*	SURNAME *sei*	PORT OF DEPARTURE *shuppatsuchi*	LENGTH OF STAY *taizai kikan*

BAGGAGE CLAIM

Where can I get my baggage?	*Te-nimotsu wa doko de uketoremasu ka?*
I can't find my baggage.	*Nimotsu ga mitsukarimasen.*
My luggage didn't come.	*Nimotsu ga dete kimasen deshita.*
My luggage is lost.	*Nimotsu ga nakunarimashita.*
My luggage is damaged.	*Nimotsu ga kowarete imasu.*

Do you have your claim tag?
Te-nimotsu hikikaeshō wa arimasu ka?

We'll deliver it to where you're staying.
Shukuhaku-saki e todokemasu.

Do you have your ticket?
Kōkūken wa arimasu-ka?

Where shall we deliver it?
Dochira e otodoke shimasho ka?

We will search for it.
Oshirabe shimasu.

We cannot locate it.
Mitsukarimasen.

It will come on the next flight.
Tsugi no bin de todokimasu.

We will replace your luggage.
Nimotsu o benshō shimasu.

We will compensate you.
Hoshōshimasu.

BAGGAGE CLAIM	CLAIM TAG /TICKET	DAMAGED	LOST
nimotsu hikitori	*te-nimotsu hikikaeshō*	*kowatete iru*	*nakushita*

GETTING TO TOKYO FROM THE AIRPORT

Getting from the airport to the heart of the city has gotten a lot more efficient. Traditionally Narita Airport was Tokyo's main international airport, and Haneda Airport was used for domestic flights. However in recent years, Haneda is being used for many more international flights, and is much closer to the city center, so it is highly recommended to fly into Haneda if you can. For transport between Haneda Airport and central Tokyo there are several options. You can take the Keikyu Line train to Shinagawa which takes 20 minutes on a regular train or 14 minutes on a rapid train and costs ¥330. This is a private train line so you cannot use your Japan Rail Pass (see page 62 and page 113). You can take the Tokyo Monorail to Hamamatsucho, which takes 25 minutes on a regular train or 17 minutes on a rapid train and costs

¥520. Use of your Japan Rail Pass is permitted. You can take a Limousine Bus which stops at various city center hotels; it takes from 30 to 60 minutes and costs ¥1,400. You buy your Limousine Bus ticket at the airport terminal counter, at an airport ticket machine, or online at klook.com. A taxi will take about 40 minutes and can cost between ¥5,000 and ¥10,000 depending on your destination and the traffic conditions.

For transport between Narita and central Tokyo, the Limousine Bus takes around 90 minutes and costs ¥3,600. There are a number of high speed train options. The Narita Express train takes about 1 hour 15 minutes to go direct to the city center and costs ¥3,070 to Tokyo Station and ¥3,250 to Shinagawa, Shibuya or Shinjuku stations. Use of your Japan Rail Pass is permitted. The Keisei Skyliner train from Narita to Ueno takes 41 minutes and costs ¥2,580. The Keisei Access Express train takes 1 hour 20 minutes to Ueno and costs ¥1,280. A regular Keisei train to Ueno takes about 80 minutes for ¥1,060 to ¥1,280. There are also early morning and evening Keisei trains called Morning Liner and Evening Liner, for which the fare between Narita and central Tokyo is ¥1,510. The Japan Rail Pass cannot be used on Keisei trains.

A taxi ride from Narita to central Tokyo is expensive due to the distance. However Narita Airport is served by fixed-fare taxis that can take you to various central destinations at fixed prices: narita-airport.jp/en/access/taxi/

Japanese airports have many stores and restaurants that you can visit before your flight. This can be great way to buy any last minute gifts or eat some of your favorite dishes—but bear in mind that many airport shops and restaurants may be closed early in the morning or late at night.

ARRIVING, GETTING AROUND AND MAKING BOOKINGS

There is a vast amount of information on the Internet to help you with arriving, getting around and booking accommodation. These include the Japan National Tourism Organization (JNTO), the Japan Travel Bureau (JTB), and IACE, all of which have slightly different website addresses depending on which country you are in.

There are many smartphone apps that you can use to enter which station you will be departing from and which station you would like to go to. Apps such as Japan Transit Planner will help you go from point A to point B and will tell you exactly how much it will cost. The app Yomiwa uses your smartphone camera to read Japanese script, which can help you navigate the stations and signs. The dictionary app called Japanese (with a red logo and white kanji) is an offline dictionary with photo lookup and a function that allows you to tap on words you have pasted into the app to see their definition.

Is there a ~ map?	*~ chizu wa arimasu ka?*
road	*dōro*
city	*shinai*
Can I reserve a hotel room here?	*Koko de hoteru no yoyaku ga dekimasu ka?*
I'd like to reserve a room in the city.	*Shinai no hoteru o yoyaku shite kudasai.*
Is there a bus to the city?	*Shinai e yuku basu wa arimasu ka?*
Where can I catch the taxi/bus?	*Takushii/Basu noriba wa doko desu ka?*
Can I reserve a ~ at this office?	*Koko de ~ no yoyaku ga dekimasu ka?*
I'd like to reserve a ~ in the city.	*Shinai no ~ o yoyaku shite kudasai.*
Western-style hotel	*hoteru*
business hotel	*bijinesu hoteru*
ryokan	*ryokan*
minshuku	*minshuku*
rental car	*rentakā*
How much is the taxi fare (to ~)?	*(~ made) Takushii de ikura kurai desu ka?*
Can I get there by bus?	*Soko made basu wa arimasu ka?*
Can I get there by train?	*Soko made densha wa arimasu ka?*
Can I get there by subway?	*Soko made chikatetsu wa arimasu ka?*
Are there sightseeing buses?	*Kankō basu wa arimasu ka?*
Where can I buy a ticket?	*Kippu wa doko de kau n'desu ka?*
Is there a/an ~ tour?	*~ no kōsu wa arimasu ka?*
half-day	*han nichi*
all-day	*ichi nichi*
morning	*gozen*
afternoon	*gogo*
Are meals included?	*Shokuji-tsuki desu ka?*
What time does it start?	*Nan-ji hatsu desu ka?*
Where does it start?	*Doko kara demasu ka?*

Most travelers choose transportation according to cost, comfort, and utility. Although comfortable, a taxi is outrageously expensive, and—in contrast to its meter—is the slowest thing around a major city during rush hour. If you're carrying a lot of luggage or if you want to be dropped off right at your destination, you may opt to take a taxi. It's certainly great for sightseeing. Nonetheless, trains and subways are unquestionably the fastest and cheapest way to go in cities, so it might be best to travel as light as possible.

I want to go by ~	~ de ikitai n'desu ga.
taxi	*takushii*
bus	*basu*
car	*kuruma*
rental car	*rentakā*
subway	*chikatetsu*
train	*densha*
express train	*kyūkō*
bullet train	*shinkansen*
plane	*hikōki*
ship	*fune*
sightseeing boat	*yūransen*
sightseeing bus	*kankō basu*
I want to walk.	*Aruite ikitai n'desu ga.*

TAKING A JR TRAIN

Except during Tokyo's rush-hour madness, trains, or *densha,* in Japan are delightful and obsessively punctual. Japan is a nation where train travel is more than simply a convenient means of transport—it's also a highly regarded popular pastime.

Japan Railways (JR), with its 20,000 kilometers of track and 25,000 daily runs, offers many travel options. Trains come in diverse configurations, from rustic simplicity to glossy sleepers aimed at honeymooners. There are local, rapid, express, and limited express trains. Falling under this last category is the *shinkansen* bullet train, running at silky-smooth high speeds, and charging fares to match its velocity.

The shinkansen and other express trains have first-class coaches called "green cars" (*guriin sha*) with lots of leg room. Rapid and local trains are generally no-frills commuter trains. Major cities have subway lines, usually connecting with JR and other railroads at major transfer stations. Trains connecting major cities are extraordinarily convenient, as well as punctual.

Ticket prices are based on distance. There is a basic fare, with surcharges for express trains, reserved seats, green car seats, and sleepers. Between Tokyo and Kyoto, travel times for plane and train are about the same, as are fares. Japanese normally travel light on trains. Hauling luggage through stations is a nightmare, and trains have little storage space for more than carry-on luggage.

The Japan Rail Pass is a great option for visitors who know they will be traveling a lot during a given time period. Passes can be bought for 7, 14 or

21 days. The passes must be bought before you leave your home country. After you arrive in Japan, you will need to exchange the purchase order that you received with the pass at a JR office. You will then be able to ride any of the JR lines without additional charge. This includes all shinkansen except the Nozomi and the Mizuho, whose cost is only partially covered by the Japan Rail Pass; to travel on these two trains you will need to purchase an additional ticket. Be sure to keep the pass safe—if you lose it, there will be no replacement. More information about the Japan Rail Pass can be found on page 113 and on the website japanrailpass.net

BUYING A TICKET FOR TRAIN AND SUBWAY

Train tickets are purchased at ticket machines for local, or basic, fares with coins or bills. Tickets can also be purchased at ticket counters for longer routes and express/first-class surcharges. JR ticket counters and travel agencies accept debit and credit cards. Subway tickets are purchased at ticket machines near the gates. It is also possible to buy day passes in most major cities—like the Tokyo Subway Ticket (tokyometro.jp/tst/en/index.html)—which can be bought from Narita and Haneda international airports and at many other locations such as convenience stores, hotels and branches of Bic Camera.

Contactless payment by swiping a debit or credit card at ticket barriers is slowly being introduced as of spring 2024, but is still the exception rather than the norm. If you are staying in Japan for more than a couple of days, buying a Pasmo Passport (pasmo.co.jp) or Welcome Suica card (jreast.co.jp/multi/en/welcomesuica/welcomesuica) both of which are aimed at tourists, is recommended. They can be loaded up with money and used for shopping, at restaurants, and for contactless payment on local (but not long-distance) transport. All you have to do is wave the card at the ticket gate and the machine will automatically deduct the amount from the card. The amount that is left can be seen as you leave the gate. Top up the money on the card at the train station using a vending machine. These cards are very convenient as they can be read through the wallet, and are universal across the country. They can also be used in many stores. Since these cards can hold a lot of money, make sure that you take extra care of them.

If you forget to charge your card and you go through the departing gate but don't have enough money to exit the station at your destination, don't worry. There's always a vending machine near the inside gates to top up the value so that you can go through the ticket barrier. Train station staff can help you through the process.

If you are interested in buying a commuter pass or a *shinkansen* ticket, the station ticket office can help you purchase the right tickets.

OPEN SEAT TICKET *jiyūseki-ken*	ONE-WAY TICKET *katamichi kippu*	BASIC FARE TICKET *jōsha-ken*	PLATFORM TICKET *nyūjō-ken*
RESERVED SEAT TICKET *shiteiseki-ken*	ROUND-TRIP TICKET *ōfuku kippu*	EXPRESS TICKET *tokkyu-ken*	FARE ADJUSTMENT *seisan*

How do I get to ~?	*~ e wa dō ittara ii desu ka?*
I can't read the fare information in Japanese.	*Nihongo no ryōkin an'nai ga yome-masen.*
How much is it to ~?	*~ made ikura desu ka?*
No tickets came out when I put money in.	*O-kane o ireta n'desu ga kippu ga demasen.*
What does this mean?	*Kore wa dō iu imi desu ka?*
Please write it here.	*Koko ni kaite kudasai.*
Please write ~ in kanji.	*~ o kanji de kaite kudasai.*
Please write ~ in romaji.	*~ o rōmaji de kaite kudasai.*

STATIONS AND EXITS

Some stations are surrounded by long underground walkways with many exits—check the website of department stores or tourist attractions beforehand to find the correct exit. On major train lines, there are screens in the trains to help you see which station you are at, and which station you are approaching. Some also list how many minutes it takes to get to all of the stations on that line. On the platforms, you will also see a map that shows which exits correlate to which stairs. Make sure to check out this map before you go out of the gates as it can save you a considerable amount of time than walking above ground. Each exit also shows major spots that can be reached from that exit. Station staff can also help point you in the right direction.

FINDING THE PLATFORM

Some stations are small and the platform can easily be found. However, in major stations like Tokyo and Shinjuku, there are more than twenty platforms. Platform information can be found all over the station to point you to the right direction. Apps like Japan Transit Planner also list the platform that each train departs.

In Japan, you wait patiently in line to get on a train, even during rush hour. Let all the people off the train before boarding and make sure to move inside the carriage as far as possible so that more people can board.

EXPRESS TRAINS VS. LOCAL TRAINS

There are various types of trains on the same line; some will stop at all stations, others only at major stations. If you are getting off at a minor station, you might need to take a local train, rather than an express train. Station signboards and apps like the Japan Transit Planner can show you which train you will need to take. The following types of trains are available in Japan from fastest to slowest: Tokkyu (Limited Express), Kyuko (Limited), Kaisoku (Rapid), and Futsu (Local).

If your departing station and the station you are headed to are both served by Limited Express, taking this train will save you a significant amount of time compared to a Local train that stops at every station.

CHANGING TO ANOTHER LINE

You will often need to change from one line to another to reach your destination. For example, in Tokyo, to get from Shinjuku to Jiyugaoka, you will need to take the Marunouchi Line from Shinjuku to Shinjuku-sanchōme and transfer to the Fukutoshin Line to get from Shinjuku-sanchōme to Jiyugaoka. Announcements are clearly made in both English and Japanese in most trains with transfer information. Once you get off the train, follow the signs to the next line. In general, if you are transferring from one JR line to another JR line, you will not need to go through the ticket gate. However, if you are going from the JR line to the subway system, you will need to exit the JR line and go through the subway ticket barrier. It is worth trying to do all of your transfers within one system (JR, Subway, Keio, etc.) in order to save on ticket fares.

TAKING A BUS

Buses usually have a front and middle door. In central Tokyo the front door is the entrance, where you pay the flat fare of ¥210, and the middle door the exit. In most other places you get on in the middle, and pay your fare when you get off at the front. When in doubt, follow the crowd to the correct door.

Where is the bus stop?	*Basutei wa doko desu ka?*
Where can I get a bus to ~?	*~ yuki no basutei wa doko desu ka?*
What bus do I take for ~?	*~ yuki no basu wa dore desu ka?*
When is the next bus to ~?	*~ yuki no tsugi no basu wa itsu desu ka?*
Does this bus go to the ~ hotel?	*Kono basu wa ~ hoteru ni tomarimasu ka?*
Does this bus go to ~?	*Kono basu wa ~ made ikimasu ka?*
Is this the right bus to ~?	*Kono basu wa ~ yuki desu ka?*
How far is it to ~?	*~ made dono kurai arimasu ka?*
Do I have to change buses?	*Basu o norikae nakereba ikemasen ka?*
Where should I get off?	*Doko de orireba ii desu ka?*
Please tell me when to get off.	*Itsu oritara ii ka oshiete kudasai.*
Can I get off at ~?	*~ de oroshite moraemasu ka?*
I'll get off at ~.	*~ de orimasu.*
Let me off here, please.	*Koko de oroshite kudasai.*
I'll get out at the next stop.	*Tsugi de orimasu.*
I'll get out at the second stop.	*Tsugi no tsugi de orimasu.*
I'll get out at the last stop.	*Shūten de orimasu.*

USING A BUS TICKET MACHINE

Tokyo bus fares are a flat fee of ¥210, but elsewhere fares are usually based on distance. For these buses, take a ticket from the dispenser next to the entrance door when you get on. The ticket has a number on it. When you get off, check the ticket number on the monitor at the front of the bus. Your fare will be displayed beneath that number. You can pay in cash, into a machine that gives change, or with a Pasmo Passport or Welcome Suica card (see page 63). As of spring 2024, there is no other form of contactless payment.

How much is the fare?	*Unchin wa ikura desu ka?*
How much is the fare to ~?	*~ made ikura desu ka?*

TAKING A TAXI

Japanese taxis are always white-glove clean. When entering and exiting, there's no need to touch the door. The driver will open and close it for you with a nifty remote lever from the driver's seat.

An empty taxi has a red indicator on the passenger-side dashboard, sometimes a mechanical flag but usually electrically lit. If a free taxi ignores you at night, it's likely because the driver is prowling for the perfect fare: an inebriated businessman who's missed the train and is heading back to the suburbs. Try the nearest luxury hotel, where taxis are always waiting.

Taxis are a safe way to travel in Japan. Most are owned by major companies, unless it says 個人 (private) on the top of the taxi. Taxis are plentiful and easy to find. Even if you are staying in a remote countryside inn, you can ask the innkeeper to call a taxi for you.

Feel free to practice your Japanese on the driver; some drivers enjoy chatting with foreigners. But just in case, have your destination written in Japanese. Tips are not expected, but if change on the fare is less than ¥50, the driver will appreciate the leftovers. Hand over your money, hesitate as the driver makes change, then say *Ē, ii desu,* "It's okay," and the driver will keep the change.

TAXI	AVAILABLE	NOT IN SERVICE	DISTANCE	DESTINATION
takushii	*kūsha*	*kaisō*	*kyori*	*yukisaki*

Go straight ahead.	*Massugu itte kudasai.*
Turn ~ at the next corner, please.	*Tsugi no kado o ~ e magatte kudasai.*
left	*hidari*
right	*migi*

Please turn left/right just up ahead.	*Sugu hidari/migi e magatte kudasai.*
Please hurry.	*Isoide kudasai.*
There's no hurry.	*Isoganakute mo ii desu.*
Could you drive slower?	*Mō sukoshi yukkuri unten shite kudasai.*
I'll get out at the intersection.	*Sono kōsaten de orimasu.*
I'll get out at the next signal.	*Tsugi no shingō de orimasu.*
Please stop over there.	*Asoko de tomete kudasai.*
Please stop here.	*Koko de tomete kudasai.*
Please let me off here.	*Koko de oroshite kudasai.*
This place is fine.	*Kono hen de ii desu.*
Stop here for a minute, please.	*Koko de chotto tomete kudasai.*
Wait a moment, please.	*Chotto matte ite kudasai.*
How much is it?	*Ikura desu ka?*
Keep the change.	*Tsurisen wa totte oite kudasai.*

Where do you want to go?
Doko e ikitai n'desu ka?

Sorry, I can't seem to find it.
Sumimasen ga mitsukaranai yō desu.

Sorry, but I don't understand.
Sumimasen ga wakarimasen.

I have to ask for directions.
Michi o kikanakutewa narimasen.

Sorry, but I can't take you there now.
Sumimasen ga ima soko e wa ikemasen.

I can/can't wait.
Matsu koto wa dekimasu/dekimasen.

WALKING AROUND

Japan is a great place to walk around as the streets are safe and there are always interesting things to catch your eye. Addresses are a little complicated so use landmarks as well as your smartphone app to help you navigate. Walk on the left side of the sidewalk. Walking is a great way to get to know a city and perhaps spot a couple of places to eat for lunch or dinner.

Try walking from one station to another instead of catching the train. Besides saving a bit on fares, you may run into some mom-and-pop stores with interesting goods. One resource if you do happen to get lost is the *kōban*, or "police box," (交番) found at regular intervals, usually on street corners. Police officers at the kōban will do their best to point you in the right direction. Many police officers speak English, especially in the bigger cities. However, it may be a good idea to carry several printed maps so that they can mark your location and destination, in case you forget their spoken directions. The kōban police officers can also help with lost property—they will ask you to fill out a form so that they can contact you if they find your lost item.

RENTING A BICYCLE

Japan is a country where getting around by bicycle is very popular. Cycling can even be a lot faster than a car depending on traffic. If you are in the Tokyo area, you can rent a bike from companies like Docomo Bike Share (docomo-cycle.jp). You should be riding on the left side of the road. Many people cycle on the sidewalks, even though it is supposed to be prohibited. You'll find fewer designated bike lanes in Japan's major cities than in other world cities, due in part to narrow roads, but the Japanese government is working on increasing the number of cycle lanes in tourist destinations and close to major stations. Despite the low incidence of crime in Japan, it's still a good idea to lock your bike when you park it.

ASKING DIRECTIONS

The easiest way to find a place is to use one of the map features on your smartphone. Using Google Maps on your computer, you could also create a map for the city you'll be traveling to and save some of its attractions or restaurants that you would want to visit.

If you need to ask directions from someone — a police officer at the kōban police box, or a member of station staff you can say:

Where is ~?   *~wa doko desu ka?*

It may be a good idea to carry a map around and have them mark the place on the map so that you can follow that visually.

FINDING SOUVENIRS OR PARTICULAR PLACES

You may often have several requests for particular souvenirs your friends, family and colleagues would like you to bring back from your trip to Japan. These can often be found in the department stores like Seibu and Takashimaya. You can also find many stylish goods from stationery to home accessories at Loft or Tokyu Hands. Prices are similar to that of other department stores in other countries, but you may find a wider array of souvenirs. If you are interested in books on Japan or manga, try the bookstores Kinokuniya or Maruzen.

If you are staying at a hotel, you can ask a member of staff where you might be able to find a particular item. In Japanese, you can say:

Where do they sell ~?   *~ wa doko de utte imasu ka?*

If you are interested in finding a particular temple or shrine; or a restaurant that specializes in certain food, you can ask one of the following questions:

Where is ~?   *~ wa doko desu ka?*
Where can I eat ~?   *~ wa doko de taberaremasu ka?*

WHERE IS IT?

The most effective way to approach a stranger is to start your request or question with *Sumimasen ga...* or "Excuse me . . ." Trail off at the end in a gentle and humble manner. The basic sentence structure for asking about a location or the whereabouts of something or someone is: (person/place/thing) *wa doko desu ka?* Using *dochira* instead of *doko* is even more polite.

Excuse me.	*Sumimasen ga...*
I'm looking for ~.	*~ o sagashite imasu.*
How do I get to ~?	*~ e iku michi o oshiete kudasai.*
Where is the ~?	*~ wa doko desu ka?*
Do you know where ~ is?	*~ wa doko ka wakarimasu ka?*
I can't find the ~.	*~ o mitsukeru koto ga dekimasen.*
Is the ~ far from here?	*~ wa koko kara tōi desu ka?*
Is the ~ close to here?	*~ wa koko kara chikai desu ka?*
Is there a ~ nearby?	*Kono chikaku ni ~ ga arimasu ka?*
Where is the closest ~ ?	*Ichiban chikai ~ wa doko desu ka?*
How should I get to ~?	*~ e wa dō ikeba ii desu ka?*
I'm trying to get to ~.	*~ e ikitai n'desu ga.*
I'm looking for ~.	*~ o sagashite imasu.*
Which way is ~?	*~ wa dochira desu ka?*
Where is the road to ~?	*~ e iku michi o oshiete kudasai.*
Is this the way to ~?	*~ e iku michi wa kore de ii desu ka?*
Is this (the) ~?	*Koko wa ~ desu ka?*
Can someone here speak English?	*Eigo o hanaseru hito wa imasu ka?*
It's supposed to be nearby.	*Kono chikaku ni aru hazu desu ga.*
I'm completely lost.	*Kanzen ni mayotte shimaimashita.*
Where are we?	*Koko wa doko desu ka?*

POLICE BOX/ STATION *kōban*	BANK *ginkō*	SUBWAY STATION *chikatetsu no eki*	TOILET/ RESTROOM *toire*
HOSPITAL *byōin*	POST OFFICE *yūbin kyoku*	TRAIN STATION *eki*	PUBLIC TELEPHONE *kōshū denwa*

BUILDING	ENTRANCE	INFORMATION DESK	CASHIER
tatemono	*iriguchi*	*an'naijo*	*reji*
ELEVATOR	EXIT	LOST AND FOUND	TICKET OFFICE
erebētā	*deguchi*	*ishitsubutsu gakari*	*kippu uriba*
(THIS) HOTEL *(kono) hoteru*	BUS STOP *basutei*	EMBASSY *taishikan*	OFFICE BUILDING *biru*
AIRPORT *kūkō*	CASTLE *shiro*	FESTIVAL *matsuri*	PARK *kōen*
ART GALLERY *garō*	CITY CENTER *shi no chushin, toshin*	LIBRARY *toshokan*	PARKING LOT *chūshajō*
BOOKSTORE *hon'ya*	CITY OFFICES *chōsha*	MOVIE THEATER *eigakan*	RESTAURANT *resutoran*
BRIDGE *hashi*	DEPARTMENT STORE *depāto*	MUSEUM *hakubutsukan*	SHRINE *jinja*

JAPAN'S GEOGRAPHY

The Japanese archipelago, or **Nihon rettō,** consists of four main islands and over 3,900 smaller islands extending to Okinawa, near Taiwan. Honshu is the largest island, home to Mt. Fuji, Tokyo, and Kyoto, as well as to most bullet train lines. It is also the site of most earthquakes. The northernmost main island, sparsely populated Hokkaido, is seen by many Japanese as a romantic rural outback, popular for skiing and honeymoons. The southernmost of the four main islands, Kyushu, was Japan's cultural connection to the outside world in ancient times, its proximity to Korea making it Japan's conduit for cultural influences from Asia. Shikoku is the smallest of the four islands, off the beaten path even for most Japanese people. Typhoons hit it regularly.

WORLD *sekai*	COUNTRY *kuni*	PREFECTURE *ken*	CITY *shi*	VILLAGE *mura*
	STATE/ PROVINCE *shū*	CAPITAL *shuto*	TOWN *machi*	CITY WARD *ku*
ISLAND *shima*	MOUNTAIN *yama*	ASIA *Ajia*	PACIFIC OCEAN *Taiheiyō*	OVERSEAS *kokugai*
	SEA, OCEAN *umi*	JAPAN *Nihon/Nippon*	SEA OF JAPAN *Nihonkai*	REGION *chihō*
INTERNATIONAL *kokusai*	DOMESTIC *kokunai*			

NAVIGATING THE STREETS

Apart from main thoroughfares, most Japanese neighborhoods are organized into numbered blocks. As these block numbers are not always sequential, it has traditionally been difficult for tourists to navigate unfamiliar districts. But with the advent of smartphone maps, which display place names in both Japanese and English, reaching your destination has become a lot easier.

If you are staying in an Airbnb apartment, for example, get your host to type in the address in Google Maps so you can easily find your way home. To retrace your steps, save the location of your starting point. If you are staying at a hotel, save the address on your phone when you get your confirmation. When I travel to Japan, I usually keep a running list of the addresses of the places I want to go to and copy and paste the addresses into Google Maps.

Sometimes though, you might need to ask for help, and the phrases below may come in useful.

How long does it take?	*Dono kurai kakarimasu ka?*
Is it near here?	*Sore wa koko kara chikai desu ka?*
Is it far from here?	*Sore wa koko kara tōi desu ka?*
Can I walk there?	*Soko e aruite ikemasu ka?*
Can I take a taxi there?	*Soko e takushii de ikemasu ka?*
Can I take a train/subway?	*Soko e densha de ikemasu ka?*
Which (train) line?	*Nani sen desu ka?*
Where do I get off?	*Doko no eki de orireba ii desu ka?*

What is the name of this street?	*Kono tōri wa nan to iimasu ka?*
Where are we right now?	*Koko wa doko desu ka?*
Should I go ~?	*~ ni ikeba ii desu ka*
straight	*massugu*
left	*hidari*
right	*migi*
Please write it here.	*Koko ni kaite kudasai.*
Please write it in Japanese.	*Sore o Nihongo de kaite kudasai.*
Please write it in romaji.	*Sore o rōmaji de kaite kudasai.*
What does this mean?	*Kore wa nan no imi desu ka?*
Where on this map am I?	*Genzaichi o shimeshite kudasai.*
Do you have maps of the area?	*Kono shūhen no chizu wa arimasu ka?*
Which way is ~?	*~ wa dochira desu ka?*
north	*kita*
south	*minami*
east	*higashi*
west	*nishi*
Are there any landmarks along the way?	*Nanika mejirushi ni naru mono ga arimasu ka?*
What is this building?	*Kono tatemono wa nan desu ka?*
What is that building?	*Ano tatemono wa nan desu ka?*
Is this the (right) building?	*Kono tatemono desu ka?*
Which building is it?	*Dono tatemono desu ka?*
Which side is it?	*Dochira-gawa desu ka?*
Which floor is it?	*Nan-kai desu ka?*
Is it open today?	*Kyō wa yatte imasu ka?*
Is it closed all day today?	*Kyō wa ichi nichi jū yasumi desu ka?*
What time does it open?	*Nan-ji ni akimasu ka?*
What time does it close?	*Nan-ji ni shimarimasu ka?*
Whom should I ask?	*Dare ni kikeba ii desu ka?*

ESSENTIAL VERBS

to go *iku*	to be lost *mayou*	to guide, show *an'nai suru*
to return home *kaeru*	to search, look for *sagasu*	to turn, curve *magaru*

LOCATION AND DIRECTION

LOCATION *ichi*	AHEAD *saki*	IN FRONT OF *mae*	ABOVE, UP, ON *ue*	INDOORS *uchi*
DIRECTION *hōkō*	NEXT TO *tonari*	IN BACK OF *ushiro*	DOWN, UNDER *shita*	OUTDOORS *soto*

THIS SIDE *kochiragawa*	RIGHT SIDE *migigawa*	LEFT SIDE *hidarigawa*	BOTH SIDES *ryōgawa*	OPPOSITE SIDE *mukōgawa*

RIGHT *migi*	STRAIGHT *massugu*	MIDDLE *man'naka*	OPPOSITE *mukai*	THE NEXT ~ *tsugi no ~*
LEFT *hidari*	BOTH WAYS *sayū*	INSIDE, CENTER *naka*	OVER THERE *mukō*	JUST BEFORE ~ *~ no temae*

ALLEY, LANE *roji*	AVENUE *ōdōri*	HIGHWAY *kōsoku dōro*	ROAD, STREET *dōro*	ROAD, ROUTE *michi*

TRAFFIC SIGNAL *shingō*	INTER-SECTION *kōsaten*	CROSSROADS *jūjiro*	SIDEWALK *hodō*	DETOUR *mawarimichi*
CORNER *kado*	T-INTER-SECTION *tsukiatari*	TRAIN CROSSING *fumikiri*	DEAD END *ikidomari*	SHORT CUT *chikamichi*

75

DECODING AN ADDRESS

Finding a specific house or building within a block can be challenging, even with a smartphone map. If your destination is written in Japanese, there are probably some hyphenated numbers followed by some kanji characters—1-4-28 XXX—in the address. Look at a nearby utility pole: there's probably a vertical sign of about a meter's length fixed to its side. Most of the sign is advertising, but at the bottom are usually hyphenated numbers and kanji characters, hopefully similar to those in your address. Use the phrases in this chapter to ask for help if you need it.

HOW ADDRESSES ARE WRITTEN

Administratively, Japan is divided into forty-seven main administrative units: one *to* (Tokyo), two *fu* (Osaka, Kyoto), one *do* (Hokkaido), and forty-three *ken,* or prefectures. Instead of street names and numbers, an address focuses in on zones-within-zones, bigger to smaller, from the prefecture to increasingly smaller units. Variations abound. It's confusing sometimes.

POSTAL CODE	PREFECTURE	CITY	WARD
yūbin bangō	*ken*	*shi*	*ku*

These are two examples of how addresses are written in Japanese:

Staying at a Hotel

If staying in the city, be prepared to spend a considerable amount of your budget on accommodations. In Tokyo, money that gets a nice and comfortable room elsewhere will get a room barely large enough for a twin bed, refrigerator, television, and an airline-sized toilet with shower. There are cheaper alternatives—capsule hotels, guest houses and Airbnb—as well as hostels. Use the Internet to look for discount deals on the accommodation you would be most comfortable staying at.

FINDING A ROOM

I'm looking for a place to stay tonight. Is anywhere available?	*Tomaru tokoro o sagashite iru n'desu ga dokoka arimasu ka?*
I'm traveling alone.	*Hitori de ryokō shite imasu.*
I'd prefer a ~.	*~ ga ii n'desu ga.*
Western-style hotel	*hoteru*
business hotel	*bijinesu hoteru*
ryokan	*ryokan*
minshuku	*minshuku*
capsule hotel	*kapuseru hoteru*
love hotel	*rabu hoteru*
youth hostel	*yūsu hosuteru*
temple lodging	*shukubō*
guest house	*gesuto hausu*
I'd like to reserve a room.	*Heya o yoyaku shitai n'desu ga.*

How much would you like to spend?	Do you want a ~?
Go-yosan wa dono kurai desho ka?	*~ ga yoshoshii desu ka?*

Can someone here speak English?   *Eigo o hanaseru hito wa imasu ka?*
Do you have a room for tonight?   *Konban heya ga arimasu ka?*
I don't have a reservation, but is there a room?   *Yoyaku shite imasen ga heya wa arimasu ka?*

My name is ~.	*Watashi wa ~ desu.*
I made a reservation.	*Yoyaku shimashita.*
Here's my confirmation.	*Kore ga kakuninsho desu.*
I'd like to ~ my reservation.	*Yoyaku o ~ shitai n'desu ga.*
confirm	*kakunin*
cancel	*kyanseru*
change	*henkō*
Can you recommend another hotel?	*Hoka no hoteru o shōkai shite kuremasen ka?*

PLACES TO STAY

Where to stay? The possibilities are many.

There are the large INTERNATIONAL HOTELS like the Hilton and the Holiday Inn. Service is impeccable, as might be expected in Japan, although room prices—room-service prices, too—can be exorbitant. For deals on accommodation, try checking online travel agents like Agoda, Expedia, Booking.com or Hotels.com. You can also check the Japanese online travel agencies JTB, IACE, and Kintetsu for hotel and airline ticket deals. An economical version of the Western-style hotel is the BUSINESS HOTEL, a no-frills utilitarian accommodation just adequate for a comfortable night's sleep, perfect for the business traveler. No room service, no porters, no wasted space. These are often found near train stations, which is convenient. You can either call these hotels directly or make the reservations online. Be sure to request a nonsmoking room if you don't smoke.

Not to be outdone for efficiency, the CAPSULE HOTEL takes conserving space almost to the absurd, stacking two compartments on top of one another, with just enough space to sleep. One literally crawls in one end, closes the "door," watches a tiny TV or goes to sleep. Designed mostly for businessmen who have missed the last train to the suburbs (or were too drunk to catch it), each capsule holds one person and does not offer much of a night's sleep, unless one is drunk. Many foreigners stay at capsule hotels for the experience or because of the price. If you wish to try this unique Japanese experience, be sure to bring noise-canceling earphones or ear plugs for better sleep. Many capsule hotels now also include basic amenities such as showers, luggage storage space and lockers, and some even offer spa facilities or slightly larger rooms. You'll need to check in and out daily though, so families might want to consider a traditional hotel room instead.

AIRBNB can provide affordable accommodation and an opportunity to stay at a local Japanese house or apartment rather than a hotel.

LOVE HOTELS are intended for brief romantic appointments, and serve an important role in Japan, since young adults usually live with their parents. Discreet and usually thematic, and sometimes kind of fun, they offer a good night's sleep late at night: beds are big and rooms are soundproof. Better still, decent late-night, all-night rates are available, as they're not much in demand after midnight.

GUEST HOUSES offer foreigners communal accommodation in major cities, usually with shared baths and cooking facilities. While they may be noisy or not too clean, they are nevertheless cheap. There are a few decent ones around, but finding them is mostly done through word of mouth.

YOUTH HOSTELS in Japan are, with some exceptions, for travelers who don't mind a little discipline in their lives. With sometimes draconian rules, Japanese hostels offer an injection of group spirit. Even more spartan and somewhat monastic in feel are *shukubō*, or rooms at temples and shrines.

The RYOKAN is a Japanese inn, usually with impeccable service and often sitting atop a hot spring. For a real Japanese experience, a *ryokan* is unrivaled. Most are expensive—on average they charge around ¥20,000 per person, and the best places charge upwards of ¥100,000—with futons for sleeping and tatami-floored rooms. Rates are per person, not per room. A full Japanese dinner, exquisitely prepared with local specialties, comes with the room. A ryokan is highly recommended if you want to experience staying in a Japanese-style establishment with traditional food—unless your plans include going out late at night, as they usually have strict curfews.

More downscale, but equally authentically Japanese, are MINSHUKU, which are family-run and much like boarding houses. Rooms are, for Japan, economical, but can be noisy, as walls are often thin. As in ryokan, each person pays the same rate, and a Japanese dinner is included. Both ryokan and minshuku can include a big communal bath which is very relaxing.

WESTERN HOTEL *hoteru*	RYOKAN *ryokan*	CAPSULE HOTEL *kapuseru hoteru*	YOUTH HOSTEL *yūsu hosuteru*	GUEST HOUSE *gesuto hausu*
BUSINESS HOTEL *bijinesu hoteru*	MINSHUKU *minshuku*	LOVE HOTEL *rabu hoteru*	TEMPLE LODGE *shukubō*	AIRBNB *eabii ando bii*

BEDDING	SHEET	DESK CLERK *furonto*	LOBBY	SECOND FLOOR
shingu	*shiitsu*	*gakari*	*robii*	*nikai*
BED *beddo*	PILLOW *makura*	MAID *mēdo, meido*	COFFEE SHOP *kōhii shoppu*	STAIRWAYS *kaidan*
FUTON *futon*	NIGHT CLOTHES *nemaki*	MANAGER *shihainin*	ELEVATOR *erebētā*	EMERGENCY EXIT *hijō guchi*
BLANKET *mōfu*	TELEPHONE *denwa*	BASEMENT *chika*	FIRST FLOOR *ikkai*	HOT SPRING *onsen*

CHECKING IN

Hotels will often have both Western- and Japanese-style rooms. When checking in, you'll inevitably be put in a Western room. You can request a Japanese-style room, but it will be about 25 percent more expensive in many cases. The total price is often counted by the number of persons in the room.

I'd like a ~	*~ o onegai shimasu.*
quiet room	*shizuka-na heya*
room with a nice view	*keshiki no ii heya*
double room	*daburu*
single room	*shinguru*
room for one/two	*hitori/futari beya*
Does it have a/an ~?	*Heya ni wa ~ ga arimasu ka?*
private bath	*o-furo*
air conditioner	*eakon*
television	*terebi*
I'll stay ~ from tonight.	*Konban kara ~ shimasu.*
one night	*ippaku*
two nights	*ni-haku*
What is the rate?	*Heyadai wa ikura desu ka?*
Do you have anything cheaper?	*Motto yasui heya wa arimasen ka?*

We're full all week.
Konshū wa zutto manshitsu desu.

We have only singles/doubles.
Hitori/Futari yō no heya shika arimasen.

Yes, we have a room.
Ee arimasu.

We're full tonight.
Konya wa manshitsu desu.

How long do you plan to stay?
Shukuhaku no yotei wa?

How much is ~?
  it altogether
  a single room
  a double room
  the service charge

~ ikura desu ka?
  zenbu de
  shinguru wa
  daburu wa
  sābisuryō wa

Are service charges included?
Sabisuryō komi desu ka?

Are there any additional expenses or costs?
Nanika betsu ni hiyō ga kakarimasu ka?

Does the price include breakfast/lunch/dinner?
Chōshoku/Chūshoku/Yūshoku-tsuki no nedan desu ka?

I'd like to pay by credit card.
Kurejitto kādo de onegai shimasu.

Do you accept credit cards?
Kurejitto kādo wa tsukaemasu ka?

Is there room service?
Rūmu sābisu ga arimasu ka?

Is there laundry service?
Sentaku no sābisu ga arimasu ka?

Is there a dry cleaning service?
Dorai kuriiningu no sābisu ga arimasu ka?

When is check-out time?
Chekku-auto wa nan-ji desu ka?

Can I get a late check-out?
Chekku-auto o osoku dekimasu ka?

Can I get the room right now?
Heya wa ima sugu toremasu ka?

Can I go to the room now?
Ima sugu heya ni hairemasu ka?

The price includes breakfast/lunch/dinner.
Chōsoku/Chūshoku/Yūshoku tsuki no nedan desu.

We don't take credit cards.
Kurejitto kādo wa uketsukete imasen.

Do you have luggage?
Nimotsu wa arimasu ka?

The room isn't ready yet.
Mada heya no yōi ga dekite imasen.

The room will be ready at ~.
~ ji ni wa heya o goriyō itadakemasu.

DURING THE STAY

Can I check my valuables? *Kichōhin o azukatte moraemasu ka?*

Can I keep this/these in your safe? *Kore o kinko ni azukatte moraemasu ka?*

I'd like to get my things from your safe. *Kinko ni azuketa mono o dashitai n'desu ga.*

Are there any messages for me? *Watashi ate no dengon ga todoite imasu ka?*

I'd like a card with the hotel's address. *Kono hoteru no jūsho o kaita kādo o kudasai.*

Where is the nearest subway station? *Koko kara ichiban chikai chikatetsu no eki wa doko desu ka?*

I'd like a wake up call at ~. *~ ji ni okoshite kudasai.*

I'd like it taken to my room. *Heya ni motte kite hoshii n'desu ga.*

Please send ~ to my room. *~ o heya ni todokete kudasai.*
   soap   *sekken*
   towels   *taoru*
   toilet paper   *toiretto pēpā*
   a blanket   *mōfu*
   ice   *kōri*

Can I leave my luggage with you? *Kono nimotsu o azukatte moraemasu ka?*

I'd like to send this baggage to ~ by delivery service. *Kono nimotsu o ~ e okuritai n'desu ga.*

I'd like you to come get it for me. *Tori ni kite hoshii n'desu ga.*

Please don't disturb me. *Okosanai de kudasai.*

Please make up this room. *Heya o sōji shite kudasai.*

Who is it? *Dare desu ka?*

One moment, please. *Chotto matte kudasai.*

Please come in. *Dōzo.*

PHONE, INTERNET AND WI-FI

Most hotels will have Internet available free or for a nominal fee. However, it will be useful to have Internet access outside of the hotel during your stay in Japan. Roaming charges to use your smartphone can be quite expensive, but there are many companies that rent out pocket Wi-Fi routers and phones. You can arrange rental either through the Internet before you leave your country or when you land at the airport.

You can easily find the companies on the Internet. I have used Global Advanced Communications and also Pururu and had great experiences. In order to avoid exorbitant data roaming fees from my usual phone company, I have my phone on airplane mode with only the Wi-Fi turned on during my stay in Japan. If your data is turned on and your phone rings, you will still be charged for the call as it had to go through the roaming feature.

In Japan there are increasing numbers of Wi-Fi hot spots. It's easier to use these if you've registered with a free Wi-Fi service such as Japan Connected or Free Wi-Fi Passport. This will give you access to more than 100,000 hot spots around Japan. Also check with your host if you're staying in an apartment—they might have a pocket Wi-Fi for you to use.

I'd like extension ~.	*Naisen ~ o onegai shimasu.*
I'd like room service.	*Rūmu sābisu o onegai shimasu.*
I'd like the front desk.	*Furonto o onegai shimasu.*
I'd like to call ~.	*~ o onegai shimasu.*
I'd like to make a long-distance call.	*Chōkyori denwa o onegai shimasu.*
I'd like to make an international call.	*Kokusai denwa o onegai shimasu.*
This is a collect call.	*Korekuto kōru de onegai shimasu.*
May I speak in English?	*Eigo de hanashite ii desu ka?*
Sorry, I don't understand.	*Sumimasen ga wakarimasen.*
I'd like to rent a pocket Wi-Fi.	*Poketto waifai o karitain desu ga.*
Could you tell me the Wi-Fi password?	*Waifai no pasuwādo o oshiete itadakemasu ka.*

STAYING AT A RYOKAN

Staying at a **ryokan** is a great way to experience staying in a traditional Japanese establishment with homemade Japanese meals, futon, and a Japanese bath. If your trip to a particular destination will involve a lot of day trips and meals out, then a ryokan might not be a good long-term base, as daily meals are often included in the price. It might be better to book a ryokan for a night or two and spend as much time as you can enjoying the ryokan facilities.

You can make reservations online for many of the bigger ryokans. You can also go through one of the Japanese travel agencies like JTB, IACE, and Kintetsu. If you are doing a side trip from Tokyo to a more rural area like Mt. Fuji, I would highly recommend staying at a ryokan.

RYOKAN ETIQUETTE

There is strict ryokan etiquette to follow. Most ryokan enforce a strict curfew and will lock the door at a certain time, expecting you to have returned to the ryokan by then.

As you enter the ryokan, you may need to take your shoes off and change into the provided slippers. There are also slippers just for the toilet. Please don't use the toilet slippers to walk around the ryokan.

Noise level is very important to keep in mind at a ryokan. Often, the walls are thin and you can hear other people. After a certain time, a quiet rule is often in place to give all patrons an opportunity to wind down and sleep.

The bath at a ryokan is often communal, which can be a little intimidating if you are not used to it. As you enter the appropriate bathroom (separated by gender), there is a changing area. You should undress completely, leave your clothes in the basket or locker in the changing area and take a small towel with you into the bathing area. In the bathing area, the first thing to do is take a shower so that you are clean before you enter the bath, which is for soaking only, not for washing.

HOT SPRING BATHING

The Japanese love getting into hot water. Japan is peppered with *onsen* hot springs, many of which have been developed into resorts.

Visiting an onsen is a unique experience. For a foreigner, the experience can be both pleasant and uncomfortable at the same time. If you've been stared at on the street, imagine the stares when you're naked at a rural hot spring resort. But soaking in an onsen, Japanese-style, is a pleasure. And afterwards, you can do as the Japanese do and take an evening stroll in the *yukata* cotton kimono provided by your hotel.

In the onsen bathtub, one soaks and communes with friends or nature. Don't take soap into the water with you. Washing is done beforehand while sitting on a stool in a row of hand-held showers and mirrors. Wash, then rinse off completely—taking care not to splatter your neighbor—before entering the bath. Note that water in the bath is very, very hot, so enter slowly.

If you have any tattoos, you may not be allowed in. However, there are some onsen that have lifted their tattoo ban. If you do have tattoos, it's a good idea to look up tattoo-friendly onsen before you depart.

PROBLEMS AT THE HOTEL

As with most places in Asia, displays of anger and indignant demands for action are neither respected nor effective in Japan. But rarely will you need to make a complaint more than once. Service is usually prompt and done with a smile.

Would you get the manager, please?	*Shihainin o yonde kudasai.*
I left the key in my room.	*Heya ni kagi o okiwasuremashita.*
I've lost my room key.	*Kagi o nakushite shimaimashita.*
Can I change rooms?	*Heya o kaetai n'desu ga.*
I'd like to change rooms.	*Heya o kaete moraemasu ka?*
Is there a larger room?	*Motto hiroi heya ga arimasu ka?*
Is there a better room?	*Mō sukoshi ii heya ga arimasu ka?*
Is there a quiet room?	*Shizuka-na heya ga arimasu ka?*
It's too small.	*Chotto chiisasugimasu.*
It's too noisy.	*Chotto urusasugimasu.*
The bathtub doesn't drain.	*Furo no mizu ga demasen.*
The lock is broken.	*Kagi ga kowarete imasu.*
The television doesn't work.	*Terebi ga tsukimasen.*
The telephone isn't working.	*Denwa ga kowarete imasu.*
The toilet doesn't flush.	*Toire no mizu ga nagaremasen.*
There's no hot water.	*Oyu ga demasen.*
There's no soap/towel.	*Sekken/Taoru ga arimasen.*
The ~ doesn't work.	*~ ga kowarete imasu.*
air conditioner	*eakon*
electric fan	*senpūki*
heater	*danbō*
electricity	*denki*
radio	*rajio*
television	*terebi*
window	*mado*
key/lock	*kagi*
I can't access the Internet.	*Intanetto ga tsunagarimasen.*

CHECKING OUT

No mysteries here. Checking out means paying the bill. These days most ryokan and minshuku take credit cards, but there may be some that still only accept cash. It's a good idea to check beforehand. Most Western-style hotels will take most cards, but not all. The hotels usually list which cards are accepted on their website. Bring two different credit cards, just in case.

I'd like to check out ~.	*~ chekku-auto shitai n'desu ga.*
soon	*sugu ni*
around noon	*hiru goro*
early tomorrow	*ashita hayaku*
tomorrow morning	*ashita no asa*
I'm checking out.	*Ima chekku-auto shimasu.*
I'd like to leave a day early.	*Ichi nichi hayaku tachitai n'desu ga.*
I'd like to stay an extra day.	*Mō ippaku shitai n'desu ga.*
I'd like to stay longer.	*Taizai o nobashitai n'desu ga.*
My bill, please.	*Shiharai o onegai shimasu.*
There may be an error on the bill.	*Seikyūsho ni machigai ga aru yō desu ga.*
Can you check it again?	*Sumimasen ga mō ichido tashika-mete kudasai.*
I'd like to get my luggage.	*Azuketa nimotsu o dashitai n'desu ga.*
I'd like to store my luggage.	*Kono nimotsu o azukatte kudasai.*
Please call a taxi.	*Takushii o yonde kudasai.*

That will/will not be a problem.	The bill and charges are correct.
Sore wa komarimasu/ kamaimasen.	*Machigai wa arimasen.*
How much longer do you wish to stay?	When will you return for your luggage?
Dore kurai taizai o nobasaremasu ka?	*Itsu nimotsu o tori ni modorimasu ka?*

Eating and Drinking

Japan has many options for eating and drinking, and for every budget, especially in cities like Tokyo and Osaka. If you would like to go to a fancy place, a reservation is a good idea. With so many restaurants in Tokyo, trying to choose one can be overwhelming. However, asking your hotel or walking around and seeing a place that is busy might be a good indication that it is a good place to try.

There are certain areas in Tokyo that specialize in a certain type of food. For example, if you go to Shinjuku or Shimbashi, you will find a lot of great yakitori places that locals go to. If you like sushi, go to Tsukiji (the former location of the fish market) or Ginza. The Internet is also a great resource for finding the best food in Japan. Or ask locals for their recommendations. You can also find a lot of restaurants on the top floors of department stores.

The food in Japan is just so good. I usually eat the minute I land and have a meal at the airport before departure as well to get my final fix! Finding a great place to eat should not be a problem.

FINDING SOMETHING TO EAT

Can you recommend a good restaurant nearby?	*Kono chikaku no ii resutoran o oshiete kudasai.*
Someplace not too expensive.	*Amari takakunai mise ga ii desu.*

Is there a/an ~ restaurant near here?	*Kono chikaku ni ~ (ryōri) no mise wa arimasu ka?*
local cuisine	*kyōdo*
Japanese	*Nihon*
French	*Furansu*
Italian	*Itaria*
Indian	*Indo*
Thai	*Tai*
Korean	*Kankoku*
Chinese	*Chūka*

I'd like to try the best local food/ cuisine.

Jimoto no meibutsu ryōri o tabetai n'desu ga.

Can you recommend a place?

O-susume no mise wa arimasu ka?

Can you make reservations for me?

Koko de yoyaku o shite moraemasu ka?

JAPANESE FOOD 1: SUSHI AND SASHIMI

SUSHI is an art in itself, and well-known even to non-natives. To watch a sushi chef serving up orders is a pleasure. There are cheap sushi shops, sometimes using circular conveyor belts called *kaiten zushi* from which you can select any plate of sushi you like the look of. Your bill is calculated by the number of empty plates you have piled up next to you. For higher quality sushi, I strongly recommend you go to a sushi bar that locals would go to. Some of my favorite places to eat sushi have been in Ginza, Tsukiji, Shibuya, and Shinjuku, all areas which have many sushi restaurants. SASHIMI is a presentation of raw seafood without sushi rice.

Good sushi is the norm in Japan and makes it hard to come back to your home country and eat the sushi there!

JAPANESE FOOD 2: YAKITORI

YAKITORI comprises various chicken parts skewered on bamboo slivers and broiled over open charcoal. Usually, patrons of *izakaya* (Japanese pubs) will wash down their yakitori with *nihonshu* (sake) or cold beer. Yakitori can be found all over Japan, often in very small restaurants where the chef cooks the yakitori in front of you. The chefs usually have specials and sometimes you can leave it up to the chef to decide what to serve you rather than ordering from a menu.

The Shimbashi and Shinjuku areas of Tokyo have lots of yakitori restaurants underneath or next to the railway tracks. They are usually filled with businessmen who are grabbing their dinner with their buddies from work. Follow the smell of charcoal—it usually leads to a yakitori place.

JAPANESE FOOD 3: NOODLES

In addition to the globally popular ramen, NOODLES in Japan include soba (made of buckwheat), and udon (thick noodles made of wheat). Ramen shops usually offer only ramen and accompaniments like *gyoza* dumplings and sautéed vegetables. You can taste various ramen from the entire country at the Ramen Museum in Shin-Yokohama. You can also see a lot of ramen places near any of the colleges, as it is a very inexpensive meal.

Soba and udon shops often have tempura (prawns or vegetables deep fried in a batter) with their noodles. Noodles are served hot or cold and every restaurant takes pride in their particular recipes.

JAPANESE FOOD 4: TONKATSU

A favorite food for many visitors is TONKATSU—a deep fried pork cutlet paired with special sauces—served with shredded cabbage, miso or pork soup, and rice. You usually can have as much rice, miso soup, and cabbage as you want. Tonkatsu restaurants can often be found on the top floors of the department stores and some specialty ones can be found in areas such as Ebisu in Tokyo. A nice cold glass of beer is the perfect accompaniment!

JAPANESE FOOD *washoku*	UNCOOKED RICE *kome*	COOKED WHITE RICE *gohan*	SOBA NOODLES *soba*

TOFU *tōfu*	PICKLED PLUM *umeboshi*	RICE CRACKERS *senbei*	RICE BALL *onigiri*
MISO SOUP *miso shiru*	PICKLES *tsukemono*	RICE CAKE *mochi*	SUSHI *sushi*
BENTO BOX LUNCH *bentō*	INSTANT RAMEN *insutanto rāmen*	SOMEN NOODLES *(thin)* *sōmen*	BEEF HOT POT *shabu-shabu*
BOX LUNCH *(sold at stations or on trains)* *ekiben*	UDON NOODLES *(thick)* *udon*	RAMEN NOODLES *rāmen*	SEAWEED *nori*
GRILLED FISH *yakizakana*	SUKIYAKI *sukiyaki*	TEMPURA *tenpura*	SEAWEED *(for stock)* *konbu*
GRILLED CHICKEN *yakitori*	PORK CUTLET *tonkatsu*	BROILED EEL *unagi*	SEAWEED *(for soup)* *wakame*

WESTERN FOOD

Western food is abundant in Japan, with many familiar Western chain restaurants such as Outback, Kentucky Fried Chicken, and McDonald's and Denny's. Family-style restaurants like Denny's often have great deals such as free-flow soft drinks. There are also many restaurants specializing in Italian, French, and Mexican food.

SOUP	SANDWICH	CURRY AND RICE	CHEESECAKE
sūpu	*sandoitchi*	*karē raisu*	*chiizukēki*
SPAGHETTI	HAMBURGER	DESSERT	PIE
supagetti	*hanbāgā*	*dezāto*	*pai*
SALAD	PIZZA	CAKE	ICE CREAM
sarada	*piza*	*kēki*	*aisu kuriimu*

ASIAN FOOD

In Japan's major cities, you can easily find Chinese, Korean, and Indian food in at a very reasonable price. Korean food has become especially popular in Japan and many restaurants offer the Korean barbecue experience. Many ethnic Asians, such as the Koreans and Chinese who have relocated to Japan, run their own restaurants, making the food served even more authentic. These Asian restaurants can be found all over Tokyo, but certain areas are known for certain types of food. If you would like authentic Korean food, you might want to go to Shin-Okubo. If you would like Chinese food, you may want to try Ikebukuro. In the Takadanobaba area, you will also find a lot of Indian, Thai, Nepalese, Pakistani and Mongolian food.

CONVENIENCE STORES

When you first get to Japan, you may be shocked at the number of convenience stores around you. At a ***konbini***, you will find drinks (both alcoholic and non-alcoholic), along with readymade food, instant noodles, batteries, pantyhose, shampoo, snacks, and batteries. If you are ever caught in the rain without an umbrella, the konbini offers ones that are only a couple of dollars. These stores are truly convenient! Furthermore, if you were to buy a pot of instant noodles, you can fill the pot with hot water at the konbini and eat it on the spot! If you buy any of the readymade food, you can have it heated up for you.

It's also a great place to try typical Japanese snacks such as *onigiri* rice balls.

The konbini is also open twenty-four hours a day, so after flying into Japan in the middle of the night, the konbini is where you'll find great food at four in the morning.

VENDING MACHINES

Japan has vending machines on every street corner and they are filled with goodies, from hot and cold drinks and ice cream to food and batteries. You can purchase items with cash, including coins and bills, or with a Welcome Suica or Pasmo Passport card (see page 63).

READING A MENU

Menus in Japanese can be read easily with a translation app. But many restaurants have a plastic version of the food (which looks exactly like the real food) in the display case at the restaurant's entrance, which you can easily point at. Some restaurants, they might offer an English menu. To ask for one, you can say:

Do you have an English menu? *Eigo no menyu arimasu ka?*

Some menus come with pictures, which can help you through the ordering process. You can also look around the restaurant to see if you see a dish that you think might be good and point to it as well. If you want to ask questions about what exactly a dish contains, these words may come in useful:

Is this ~? *Kore wa ~ desu ka?*
beef	*gyūniku*
pork	*butaniku*
chicken	*chikin, toriniku*
vegetables	*yasai*
fish	*sakana*

ASKING A SERVER FOR HELP

Trying different types of food in a new country is both fun and scary at the same time. You could be apprehensive that you might order something very exotic that you are unused to. Use some of the following phrases can help you through the process of selecting an item that's within your comfort zone.

Do you have ~?	*~ ga arimasu ka?*
I'll have ~.	*~ o kudasai.*
I don't want ~.	*~ wa kekkō desu.*
What's the house specialty?	*Koko no o-susume ryōri wa nan desu ka?*
Is there a set menu?	*Setto menyū wa arimasu ka?*
I'll take what you recommend.	*Anata no o-susume ni shimasu.*
I'll have that.	*Sore o moraimasu.*
Give me the same as that.	*Are to onaji mono o kudasai.*
How long does it take?	*Dono kurai kakarimasu ka?*
How many minutes will it take?	*Nan-pun kurai de dekimasu ka?*
Can I have it right away?	*Sugu dekimasu ka?*
How do you eat this?	*Tabekata o oshiete kudasai.*

If eating with Japanese companions (or even if not), say *itadakimasu* just before starting the meal. When finished, saying *gochisōsama deshita* will be appreciated by your host (and the chef). Say both with sincerity.

OTHER FOOD OPTIONS

With different allergies and perhaps food items you don't care for, here are some phrases that might come in handy if you need to decipher whether you can (or want to) order the dish or not. For Muslim travelers, it would be best to do some research online beforehand to find Halal-certified restaurants.

I have allergies to ~.   I cannot eat ~.

~ no arerugii ga arimasu.   ~ ga taberaremasen.

shellfish	*kairui*
peanuts	*piinattsu*
prawns	*ebi*
gluten	*komugi, guruten*
meat	*niku*
pork	*butaniku*
lard	*rādo*

ARRIVING AT A RESTAURANT

Is there a table for ~ people?	*~ nin desu ga seki wa toremasu ka?*
I have a reservation.	*Yoyaku shite arimasu.*
Where is the restroom?	*Toire wa doko desu ka?*
May I use your restroom?	*Chotto toire o karitai n'desu ga.*
I'd like to see a menu, please.	*Menyū o misete kudasai.*
Is there an English menu?	*Eigo no menyū wa arimasu ka?*
A little more time, please.	*Mō sukoshi matte kudasai.*

We haven't any tables.
Manseki desu.

Are you ready to order?
Go-chūmon wa okimari desu ka?

Just yourself?
Ohitori desu ka?

Do you want something to drink?
Onomimono wa ikaga desu ka?

How many in your group?
Nan-mei sama desu ka?

I'll return when you're ready to order.
Go-chūmon ga kimattara mata ukagaimasu.

ORDER *chūmon*	MEAL *shokuji*	RESERVED *yoyakuseki*	EATING OUT *gaishoku*	NO SMOKING *kin'en*
FOOD *tabemono*	MENU *menyū*	SERVER *resutoran sutaffu*	SECOND SERVING *o-kawari*	SHARE A TABLE *aiseki*

BREAKFAST *chōshoku,* *asa gohan*	LUNCH *chūshoku,* *hiru gohan*	DINNER *yūshoku,* *yū gohan,* *yūhan*	SET MENU (WESTERN FOOD) *setto*	SET MENU (JAPANESE FOOD) *teishoku*

ON THE TABLE

ASHTRAY *haizara*	MATCHES *matchi*	HAND TOWEL *oshibori*	NAPKIN *napukin*
JAPANESE WARE *washokki*	JAPANESE TEAPOT *kyūsu*	RICE BOWL, TEA CUP *chawan*	CHOPSTICKS *hashi*
JAPANESE TEA CUP *yunomi*	LACQUER SOUP BOWL *(o-)wan*	TRAY *bon*	WOODEN CHOPSTICKS *waribashi*
WESTERN WARE *yōshokki*	DRINKING GLASS *koppu*	DISH, PLATE *sara*	KNIFE *naifu*
COFFEE CUP *kōhii kappu*	WINEGLASS *(wain) gurasu*	FORK *fōku*	SPOON *supūn*

DRINKS, HOT AND COLD

I'd like a drink first.	*Mazu nani ka nomitai n'desu ga.*
Do you have ~?	*~ ga arimasu ka?*
I'll have ~.	*~ o kudasai.*
I don't want ~.	*~ wa kekkō desu.*

DRINK *nomimono*	DECAF COFFEE *kafein nuki no kōhii*	LEMON TEA *remon tii*	COCOA *kokoa*

COLD *(drink, adj.)* *tsumetai*	ICED COFFEE *aisu kōhii*	MILK TEA *miruku tii*	LEMONADE *remonēdo*
HOT *(drink, adj.)* *atsui*	TEA *o-cha*	COLA *kōra*	JUICE *jūsu*
ICE *kōri*	GREEN TEA *ryoku-cha*	MILK *miruku*	APPLE JUICE *ringo jūsu*
WATER *mizu*	OOLONG TEA *ūron-cha*	SKIM MILK *sukimu miruku*	ORANGE JUICE *orenji jūsu*
HOT WATER *sayu*	BARLEY TEA *mugi-cha*	LOW FAT MILK *rōfatto miruku*	PINEAPPLE JUICE *painappuru jūsu*
COFFEE *kōhii*	BLACK TEA *kōcha*	COLD MILK *tsumetai miruku*	TOMATO JUICE *tomato jūsu*
AMERICAN COFFEE *amerikan kōhii*	ICED TEA *aisu tii*	HOT MILK *hotto miruku*	

DRINKING ALCOHOL

If drinking alcohol with Japanese people, never fill your own glass—someone else will keep it full. Your responsibility is to keep other glasses filled. Doing so will help bring you into the group. Drinking in Japanese culture helps to strengthen relationships both in friendship and business, and there are many establishments for evening drinks, from *sunakku bā*—much like Western lounges—to *nomi-ya*, more traditional Japanese drinking establishments.

I'd like ~.	*~o kudasai.*
I'll have ~.	*~ ni shimasu.*
I don't want ~.	*~ wa kekkō desu.*
Do you have ~?	*~ ga arimasu ka?*
Cheers!	*Kanpai!*

ALCOHOLIC DRINKS *sake*	BEER *biiru*	WINE *wain*	SWEET *amakuchi no*
JAPANESE SAKE *nihonshu*	WHISKY AND WATER *mizuwari*	RED *aka*	DRY *karakuchi no*
SAKE *sake*	ON THE ROCKS *on za rokku*	WHITE *shiro*	SHOCHU *shōchū*
SPECIAL RICE WINE *seishu*	BRANDY *burandē*	ROSÉ *roze*	CHAMPAGNE *shanpan, shanpen*

ORDERING MORE

May I have a little more, please?	*Mō sukoshi itadakemasu ka?*
May I have some more, please?	*Mō sukoshi kudasai.*
Do you have a breakfast special?	*Mōningu sābisu wa arimasu ka?*
I'll have the breakfast special.	*Mōningu sābisu o onegai shimasu.*
A second helping.	*Okawari.*

BREAKFAST

The traditional Japanese breakfast is made up of rice, fish, miso soup, and raw egg. Western-style breakfasts are also common, although they often have Japanese twists such as a side salad or a bowl of corn soup. Most restaurants serving breakfast have decently priced "morning sets" that may include toast, eggs, salad, and coffee. McDonald's or Starbucks are ubiquitous across the country. The drink sizes are smaller than in the US.

CORN FLAKES *kōn furēku*	BACON AND EGGS *bēkon eggu*	PANCAKES *hotto kēki*	BREAD ROLL *rōrupan*
OATMEAL *ōtomiiru*	SAUSAGE AND EGGS *sōsēji to tamago*	JAM *jamu*	TOAST *tōsuto*
HAM AND EGGS *hamu eggu*	CHEESE OMELET *chiizu omuretsu*	BREAD *pan*	SALAD *sarada*

DAIRY PRODUCTS

DAIRY PRODUCTS *nyūseihin*	MILK *(cow)* *gyūnyū*	BUTTER *batā*	CHEESE *chiizu*
FRESH CREAM *nama kuriimu*	MILK *(general)* *miruku*	MARGARINE *māgarin*	YOGURT *yōguruto*

EGGS

EGG *tamago*	SOFT-BOILED EGG *hanjukutamago*	FRIED EGG *medamayaki*	OMELET *omuretsu*
BOILED EGG *yudetamago*	HARD-BOILED EGG *katayudetamago*	SCRAMBLED EGGS *iritamago*	RICE OMELET *omuraisu*

FRUIT

FRUIT *kudamono, furutsu*	GRAPEFRUIT *gurēpufurūtsu*	MANDARIN ORANGE *mikan*	PINEAPPLE *painappuru*
APPLE *ringo*	GRAPES *budō*	PAPAYA *papaia*	PLUM *sumomo, puramu*
APRICOT *anzu*	KIWI *kiuifurūtsu*	PEACH *momo*	RAISINS *hoshi-budō*
BANANA *banana*	LEMON *remon*	PEAR *yōnashi*	RASPBERRY *ki'ichigo*
CHERRY *sakuranbo*	ORANGE *orenji*	JAPANESE PEAR *nashi*	STRAWBERRY *ichigo*
CHESTNUT *kuri*	MELON *meron*	PERSIMMON *kaki*	WATERMELON *suika*

VEGETABLES

VEGETABLE *yasai*	BAMBOO SHOOTS *takenoko*	CARROT *ninjin*	CORN *tōmorokoshi*
ASPARAGUS *asuparagasu*	BEAN SPROUTS *moyashi*	CAULIFLOWER *karifurawā*	CUCUMBER *kyūri*
AVOCADO *abokado*	CABBAGE *kyabetsu*	CELERY *serori*	EGGPLANT *nasu*
GREEN PEPPER *piiman*	LOTUS ROOT *renkon*	ONION *tamanegi*	SPINACH *hōrensō*
DAIKON RADISH *daikon*	MUSHROOM *kinoko*	PEAS *endōmame*	SQUASH *kabocha*
LETTUCE *retasu*	SHIITAKE MUSHROOM *shiitake*	POTATO *jagaimo*	TOMATO *tomato*

SEAFOOD

FISH *sakana*	EEL *unagi*	PRAWN *kuruma ebi*	SHRIMP *ama ebi*
GRILLED FISH *yakizakana*	HALIBUT *ohyō*	RED SNAPPER *tai*	SHRIMP, PRAWN *ebi*
ABALONE *awabi*	LOBSTER *ise ebi*	SALMON *sake*	SQUID, CUTTLEFISH *ika*
BONITO *katsuo*	MACKEREL *saba*	SCALLOP *hotate*	TROUT *masu*
CLAM *hamaguri*	OCTOPUS *tako*	SEAWEED *wakame*	TUNA *maguro*

CRAB	OYSTER, CLAM	SHELLFISH	SEA URCHIN
kani	*kaki*	*kai*	*uni*

MEAT

MEAT	STEAK	LAMB	TURKEY
niku	*sutēki*	*kohitsuji*	*shichimenchō*
BACON	GROUND BEEF	LIVER	SAUSAGE
bēkon	*gyū no hikiniku*	*rebā*	*sōsēji*
BEEF	SALISBURY STEAK	MUTTON	CHICKEN
gyūniku	*hanbāgu*	*maton*	*toriniku*
JAPANESE BEEF	HAM	PORK	WHALE
wagyū	*hamu*	*butaniku*	*kujira*
WELL-DONE	BAKED	FRIED	SMOKED
yoku yaketa	*yaita*	*ageta*	*kunsei ni shita*
MEDIUM	BARBECUED	GRILLED	STUFFED
midiamu	*jikabi de yaita*	*amiyaki ni shita*	*tsumemono ni shita*
RARE	BOILED/STEWED	SAUTÉED	RAW
rea	*nikonda*	*itameta*	*nama no*

CONDIMENTS

WASABI	KETCHUP	PEPPER	SOY SAUCE
wasabi	*kechappu*	*koshō*	*shōyu*
GARLIC	MAYONNAISE	CHILI PEPPER	SUGAR
nin'niku	*mayonēzu*	*tōgarashi*	*satō*
GINGER	MUSTARD	SALT	VINEGAR
shōga	*karashi*	*shio*	*su*

Is there any ~?　　　　　　*~ wa arimasu ka?*
Please bring me ~.　　　　　*~ o motte kite kudasai.*

PROBLEMS

I'm sorry, but I can't eat this.	*Sumimasen ga kore wa taberaremasen.*
I didn't order this.	*Kore wa chūmon shite imasen.*
My order hasn't come yet.	*Ryōri ga mada kite imasen.*

TASTE	DELICIOUS	OILY	SOUR	STRONG *(drink)*
aji	*oishii*	*aburakkoi*	*suppai*	*koi*
BITTER	HOT, SPICY	SALTY	SWEET	WEAK *(drink)*
nigai	*karai*	*shoppai*	*amai*	*usui*

MISCELANEOUS RESTAURANT VOCABULARY

RESTAURANT, RESTAURANT BILL	APPETIZER	CAFETERIA	DRINK AFTER MEAL
resutoran, kanjō	*zensai, ōdoburu*	*shokudō*	*shokugo no nomimono*
MORNING SERVICE	MIDNIGHT SNACK	COFFEE SHOP	DRINK BEFORE MEAL
mōningu sābisu	*yashoku*	*kissaten*	*shokuzenshu*

PAYING THE BILL

In most places you will be able to use credit or debit cards, Welcome Suica or Pasmo Passport cards (see page 63), or other contactless payment such as Apple Pay or scanning a QR code. Cash is still almost always accepted.

Often on restaurant tables, there are cylindrical holders where bills are placed. In Japan, you pay the bill at the cash register near the entrance rather than at the table. There is no need for a tip.

It was delicious.	*Oishikatta desu.*
It was more than I could finish.	*Ōsugite nokoshimashita.*
Does the bill include the service charge?	*Kono kanjō ni sābisu-ryō wa fukumarete imasu ka?*
Can I have the bill, please?	*Okaikē, onegai shimasu.*
Do you accept credit cards?	*Kurejitto kādo wa tsukaemasu ka?*
Excuse me, what is this amount for?	*Sumimasen ga kore wa nan no kingaku desu ka?*

CHAPTER 7

Telephone, Internet and Social Media

The easiest and cheapest way to ensure you are able to make phone calls, send messages, and access the Internet during your trip to Japan is to either rent a phone or a pocket Wi-Fi (see overleaf for more details).

If you plan to bring your laptop, first check that it is compatible with Japan's unique electric current (100V AC, 60 Hz in western Japan, 50 Hz in eastern Japan). Most laptops can be used without difficulty. However, you'll need either a plug adaptor or transformer to fit your three-pronged plug into Japan's two-pin wall sockets.

Most modern hotels offer free Internet. In general, Internet service is available in your room if you bring your own laptop, tablet, or smartphone. Internet cafés are common in major cities, and many coffee shops offer wireless service for customers. *Manga kissa* (twenty-four-hour cafés offering manga to read) offer Internet as well as ample reading material and, in a pinch, can also double up as cheap accommodation.

SMARTPHONES AND INTERNET

I'd like to rent a pocket Wi-Fi.	*Poketto waifai o karitai n'desu ga.*
I'd like to rent a phone.	*Keitai o karitai n'desu ga.*
Do you have free Wi-Fi?	*Muryō no waifai wa arimasu ka?*
Could you tell me the Wi-Fi password?	*Waifai no pasuwādo o oshiete itadakemasu ka?*
Can you give me your email address?	*Mēruadoresu o oshiete itadakemasu ka?*
Can you message me?	*Messēji o itadakemasu ka?*
Can I message you?	*Messēji o okutte mo ii desu ka?*
Can you give me your username?	*Yūzā-mei o oshiete itadakemasu ka?*
Can I follow you?	*Forō shite mo ii desu ka?*
Please follow me on Instagram.	*Watashi no insutaguramu o forō shite kudasai.*
My account name is ~.	*Watashi no akaunto-mei wa ~ desu.*

TELEPHONE LANGUAGE

Hello?	***Moshi-moshi.***
Hello, is this ~?	***Moshi-moshi. ~-san desu ka?***
May I speak to ~?	***~-san o onegai shimasu.***
Is ~ there?	***~-san wa irasshaimasu ka?***
This is ~.	***~ desu.***
May I speak in English?	***Eigo de hanashite ii desu ka?***
Please give me someone who speaks English.	***Eigo no hanaseru hito o onegai shimasu.***
This is an emergency.	***Kinkyū desu.***
I'd like extension ~.	***Naisen ~ o onegai shimasu.***
Sorry, I don't understand anything.	***Sumimasen ga zenzen wakarimasen.***
I don't speak Japanese.	***Nihongo o hanasemasen.***
My telephone number here is ~.	***Watashi no denwa bangō wa ~ ban desu.***
I'll call again later.	***Mata ato de denwa shimasu.***

POCKET WI-FI ROUTERS

Pocket Wi-Fi routers, which allow you to access the Internet virtually anywhere in Japan, can easily be rented in your country before departure or at the airport when you arrive. You can also rent them from Japanese companies like Pururu and Advanced Global Communications, which have websites in English; such companies usually require you to reserve the pocket Wi-Fi with at least one week's notice. You can also arrange to either pick it up at the airport or at your hotel when you arrive.

When ordering a pocket Wi-Fi you will need to consider how much data you will use per day and the speed. Prices increase with speed and the amount of data you can use. However, if you get the more inexpensive plans and you wind up using more data than allotted, your speed may be slowed down for twenty-four hours as a penalty.

USEFUL APPS

In addition to your usual apps, some that I would recommend include Japan Transit Planner, which gives you real time information on trains and subways, and a Japanese translator. My favorite dictionary app is called Japanese (with the red icon and white kanji). You can also draw the kanji on the app to learn how to pronounce the word. The dictionary is very good and does not require Internet connection when you are using it. I would also recommend downloading your airline's app so that you can check in and see your seats easily. I also have an app to get the yen to dollar conversion so that I don't have to go on the Internet each time for the exchange rate. The most popular messaging app in Japan is Line which has a multitude of features, and is a must when communicating with your Japanese friends.

MESSAGING TO MEET JAPANESE FRIENDS

The most popular smartphone app for messaging in Japan is Line. Having telephone conversations on the bus, train or subway is frowned upon in Japan, so if you are on public transport and need to communicate with your friends to tell them you are running late, then messaging is the best option.

When you message your Japanese friends to meet up with them, make sure that you have agreed an exact location to meet, especially if it's at a large train station with many different exits. For example, if you are going to meet at a station ticket barrier (***kaisatsu guchi***) you may also need to specify which exit—west gate (***nishi guchi***), east gate (***higashi guchi***), south gate (***minami guchi***) or north gate (***kita guchi***).

CHAPTER 8
Traveling Around Japan

If you are planning to travel to various places in Japan, the most economical way is to buy a Japan Rail Pass (see page 62 and page 113). It is similar to the European Eurail Pass where you can get on unlimited number of trains for a given period of time. The Japan Rail Pass can be bought on the Internet, **prior** to leaving your home country. You will not be able to buy it in Japan.

Japanese trains are extremely efficient and the ***shinkansen*** bullet trains are very comfortable. Some bullet trains have food trolleys, but not all, so make sure you bring enough food and drink with you for your journey.

MAP OF JAPAN

Area: 377,972 sq.km.
Population: 127.1 million
Population density: 340 people/sq.km.
Average lifespan: male, 80; female, 86
Per capita GDP: $38,550 (2017)

Japan is divided up into 43 administrative districts called prefectures, which are somewhat like states in the United States. A more detailed map is shown on pages 6–7.

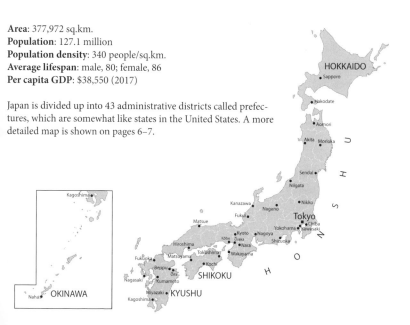

111

GEOGRAPHICAL LANDMARKS

Geographical landmarks tend to become tourist destinations in themselves—a westernmost cape is visited because it is the westernmost cape, not necessarily because it's especially pretty. Peninsulas, islands, hills, and waterfalls can become landmarks—"famous," as it's often translated in English—for local people.

GEOGRAPHY *chiri*	DESERT *sabaku*	ISLAND *shima*	MOUNTAIN *yama*	VALLEY *tani*
COAST, SEA SHORE *kaigan*	FOREST *mori*	LAND *riku*	MOUNTAIN RANGE *sanmyaku*	SLOPE, INCLINE *saka*
HILL *oka*	FOREST, WOODS *shinrin*	PENINSULA *hantō*	MOUNTAIN SUMMIT *chōjō*	VOLCANO *kazan*
BAY, GULF *wan*	HOT SPRINGS *onsen*	POND *ike*	SEA, OCEAN *umi*	STRAITS *kaikyō*
HARBOR *minato*	LAKE *mizu'umi*	RIVER *kawa*	MARSH *numa*	WATERFALL *taki*
COUNTRY *kuni*	STATE, PROVINCE *shū*	CITY *shi*	TOWN *machi*	VILLAGE *mura*

BUYING A SHINKANSEN BULLET TRAIN TICKET

You can buy a shinkansen ticket easily at the station at the *Midori no Madoguchi*, or "Green Window." You will need to determine which type of shinkansen you will be riding. The Kodama is a local shinkansen. If you are getting off at a minor train station, you would probably need to be on the Kodama. Hikari stops at some of the minor stations and Nozomi only stops at the major stations. For example, if you are going from Tokyo to Kyoto, you probably want to catch the Nozomi. On the Nozomi, the train ride would be around 2 hours and 18 minutes. On the Hikari, it would be 2 hours and 50 minutes and on the Kodama, it would be around 4 hours.

You will also need to determine if you would like a regular seat or a green seat, which is like business class. You may also want to get a reserved seat, especially if you are traveling during peak hours.

JAPAN RAIL PASS

If traveling around the country by train sounds immensely enticing, consider a one-, two- or three-week Japan Rail (JR) Pass. Once a pass has been activated it must be used within the time period specified, so you might want to plan it so that you travel during one week and then you are in one city for the rest of the time. To get your money's worth you need to travel long distances or very frequently within the allotted time period. A JR Pass entitles one to unlimited travel on all (and only) JR trains, including the shinkansen. Passes are available for ordinary and first-class seats, with surcharges for sleeping berths and private compartments. A JR pass, however, won't get you onto a train belonging to one of the myriad private railroads.

In order to be eligible to purchase the JR pass, you must be a foreign tourist visiting Japan abroad for sightseeing or a Japanese national living outside of Japan. You may purchase JR passes in the form of 7, 14, or 21 days. You may also buy the Ordinary seats or on the Green seats. Green seats are first class seats. As of April 2024, an Ordinary 7-day ticket costs ¥50,000, whereas the Green 7-day ticket costs ¥70,000.

You must plan ahead: the pass must be paid for prior to arrival in Japan. The selling agent will issue a voucher, which you can exchange for the pass at JR centers in most major JR train stations. In order to find these ticket offices, you can ask:

Where's the JR ticket office?   ***Midori no madoguchi wa doko desu ka?***

Because these offices deal with JR Passes frequently, most staff speak some English. If you show them the voucher here, they will know exactly what you are looking for.

The JR Pass is valid for railways (limited express trains, express trains, rapid and local trains), buses, and ferry boats. It covers travel on all shinkansen except for the Nozomi and Mizuho, for which you will need to buy an extra ticket.

More information about the Japan Rail Pass can be found on page 62 and on the website japanrailpass.net.

BUYING TICKETS FOR LOCAL PUBLIC TRANSPORT

The most convenient way to buy a ticket for travel on public transport within a city is to initially buy a Welcome Suica or Pasmo Passport card (see page 63), which you can load up with money before you travel, and simply touch to an electronic reader to pay your fare. These cards can be used on both JR train lines and the subway system.

BUYING TICKETS FOR LONG-DISTANCE TRAINS

Pasmo Passport or Welcome Suica cards (see page 63) cannot be used on long-distance trains. You will need to buy a ticket before you get on the train. The conductor will come through the carriage at regular intervals to check tickets. If you've bought the wrong ticket, you may need to pay extra to settle the difference.

TICKET MACHINES FOR INTERCITY TRAVEL

Each train station has ticket machines and a map above it to show how much it is from one point to the other. However, if you have a Pasmo Passport or Welcome Suica card (see page 63) and the Japan Transit Planner app, you can bypass this area and go straight to the ticket entrance. This can save you a lot of time and hassle. The app can tell you exactly which line to take and which platform you should be on.

USEFUL PHRASES FOR TRAIN TRAVEL

Can someone here speak English?	*Eigo o hanaseru hito wa imasu ka?*
I'd like to go to ~.	*~ ni ikitai n'desu ga.*
How do I get to ~?	*~ e wa dō ittara ii desu ka?*
How much is it to ~?	*~ made ikura desu ka?*
How much from here to ~?	*Koko kara ~ made ikura desu ka?*
What time is the next train?	*Tsugi no densha wa nan-ji desu ka?*
Is there a train leaving around ~?	*~ ji goro no densha wa arimasu ka?*
What times is the train for ~ ?	*~ yuki no densha wa nan-ji ni de-masu ka?*
When is the ~ to ~?	*~ yuki no ~ wa nan-ji desu ka?*
next train	*tsugi no densha*
first train	*shihatsu densha*
last train	*shūden*

How about the next train?	*Tsugi no densha wa dō desu ka?*
How about a later time?	*Motto osoi jikan wa dō desu ka?*
How about an earlier time?	*Motto hayai jikan wa dō desu ka?*
Any time is fine with me.	*Nan-ji de mo kamaimasen.*
How long does the trip take?	*Dono kurai jikan ga kakarimasu ka?*
Do I have to change trains?	*Norikae ga arimasu ka?*
Where do I change trains?	*Doko de norikae desu ka?*
Can I stop along the way?	*Tochū de noriori dekimasu ka?*
Is there an express?	*Kyūkō wa arimasu ka?*
Is there a sleeper?	*Shindaisha wa tsuite imasu ka?*
What track does it leave from?	*Nan-ban sen kara demasu ka?*
I'd like to reserve a seat on that train.	*Sono densha no zaseki o yoyaku shitai n'desu ga.*
I'd like to change this ticket to first-class.	*Kono kippu o guriin-sha ni kaetai n'desu ga.*
I'd like to ~ my reservation.	*Yoyaku o ~ shitai n'desu ga.*
confirm	*kakunin*
cancel	*kyanseru*
change	*henkō*
I'd like a refund, please.	*Haraimodoshi o onegai shimasu.*
A ticket to ~, please.	*~ made kippu o ichi-mai kudasai.*
One ticket	*Ichi-mai*
Two tickets	*Ni-mai*
One way	*Katamichi*
round trip	*ōfuku*
regular	*futsū-sha*
first-class	*guriin-sha*
open seating	*jiyū-seki*
reserved seating	*shitei-seki*
window seat	*madogawa no seki*
aisle seat	*tsūrogawa no seki*
two adjacent seats	*tsuzuite iru seki o futatsu*
in the front of the car	*mae no hō no seki*
in the back of the car	*ushiro no hō no seki*
nonsmoking seat	*kin'en-seki*
smoking seat	*kitsuen-seki*
seat with legroom	*ichiban hiroi seki*
seat as far as possible away from the smoking seats	*dekiru dake kitsuen-seki kara tōi seki*

115

That train is full.
Kono ressha wa manseki desu.

There are seats on the ~ train.
-ni seki ga arimasu ga.

How about the next train?
Tsugi no densha wa dō desu ka?

Than are only ~ on that train.
Kono ressha wa ~ dake desu.

Smoking or nonsmoking?
Kitsuen-seki, kin'en-seki no dochira ni shimasu ka?

There are no ~ [on that train].
-wa arimasen.

READING JAPANESE TRAIN TERMS

(快速) RAPID TRAIN faster than local 快速列車	⊠ FIRST-CLASS non-reserved seats 自由席グリーン車	🖪★ LIMITED EXPRESS sleeper coach 寝台特急
急行 ORDINARY EXPRESS faster than local/rapid 急行列車	⊠ FIRST-CLASS reserved seats 指定席グリーン車	🖪★ ORDINARY EXPRESS sleeper coach 寝台急行
特急 LIMITED EXPRESS faster than ordinary express 特急列車	STANDARD CAR nonreserved/reserved 自由指定席	A寝 SLEEPER CAR first-class cabins A寝台
L LIMITED EXPRESS L faster than limited エル特急	全 STANDARD CAR all reserved 全指定席	B寝 SLEEPER CAR second-class cabins B寝台

AT THE STATION

Interior station signs in major cities often have English words or at least roman alphabet versions of Japanese words. Signs for train lines also have particular color schemes, which you will become familiar with, even if you can't read the Japanese script.

Where are the shinkansen tracks?	*Shinkansen no hōmu wa doko desu ka?*
Which train goes to ~?	*~ yuki wa dore desu ka?*
What track is the ~ Line?	*~ sen wa nan-bansen desu ka?*
Where is the ~ Line?	*~ sen wa doko desu ka?*
Is this the platform for the ~ Line?	*~ sen wa kono hōmu desu ka?*
Is this the right platform for the train to ~?	*~ yuki no densha wa kono hōmu desu ka?*
What track does the train for ~ leave from?	*~ yuki no densha wa nan-bansen kara demasu ka?*
Is this the train for ~?	*Kono densha wa ~ yuki desu ka?*
Is this train a local/limited express?	*Kono densha wa kakueki/tokkyū desu ka?*
Is this the subway to ~?	*Kono chikatetsu wa ~ yuki desu ka?*

It's a different train.
Chigau densha desu.

It's on platform number
~bansen desu

It's on a different platform.
Chigau hōmu desu.

It's already left.
Mō demashita.

It's on the next platform.
Tonari no hōmu desu.

117

TIMETABLE	DESTINATION	AWAY FROM TOKYO	RAPID TRAIN
jikokuhyō	*yukisaki*	*kudari*	*kaisoku*
ARRIVALS	BOUND FOR ~	TRANSFER	LOCAL EXPRESS
tōchaku	*~yuki*	*norikae*	*junkyū*
ARRIVAL TIME	IN DIRECTION OF ~	TERMINATES AT ~	EXPRESS TRAIN
tōchaku jikoku	*~ hōmen*	*~ domari*	*kyūkō*
DEPARTURES	VIA ~	LOCAL TRAIN	LIMITED EXPRESS
hassha	*~ keiyu*	*kakueki teisha, futsū*	*tokkyu*
DEPARTURE TIME	TOWARDS TOKYO		BULLET TRAIN
hassha jikoku	*nobori*		*shinkansen*

NAVIGATING THE STATION

Mastering the large stations that serve as major transfer points is sometimes intimidating, especially because of long hikes between connections and endless stairways and escalators to everywhere. (It's recommended not to try to carry more than one large piece of luggage through such stations.) Shinjuku and Tokyo stations, for example, are especially confusing labyrinths, even to the initiated. But stations are usually well-marked, with signs in English.

TRAINS: JR stations are generally above ground and entered from street level. Entrances/exits are usually identified by compass points, such as *higashi guchi*, or "east gate" (see page 109). (At Tokyo Station, main gates are also identified as the Yaesu or Marunouchi sides.) Ticket machines and coin lockers are often near entrances. Local JR train lines, as well as subways, are identified by name and color. (Trains of the same line going in opposite directions do not always share the same platform; double-check the signs.)

Barring earthquakes and typhoons, trains in Japan are almost always punctual down to the minute, adhering to strict timetables, copies of which are mounted in poster form on platforms.

SUBWAYS: Despite the often convoluted nature of their layouts, navigating subway stations is easy, for they are extremely well-marked with signs and maps, and also have English signage. In Tokyo, subway stations usually have a number of exits—marked A1, A2, etc.—leading up to several street-level places, including department store interiors.

During rush hours on the subway certain cars are reserved exclusively for women, to reduce the number of incidences of groping. These cars, along with the timings that they are in effect are marked on the train and platform.

AVOID THE CROWDS

Avoid intercity train travel during the holiday seasons, when shinkansen bullet trains run at 100 to 200 percent capacity and you may not be able to get a seat. On the other hand, urban Tokyo during the holiday season becomes a delight, as the city and its trains are markedly less crowded.

You should also avoid urban subways and commuter trains during morning and evening rush hours, unless you enjoy being crushed. If a train looks full to the brim, the next one may have more room. Also try the first and last car of a train—they tend to be less crowded.

ON THE TRAIN

Overall, traveling by train in Japan is generally a pleasure. On long-distance expresses, seats are usually very comfortable. Local train seats, unfortunately, can be a bit of a squeeze for tall people.

Eating on the long-distance trains is perfectly acceptable, even encouraged by JR; some trains even have trays that fold out of the backs of seats, airplane-style. Food and drinks, including beer, can be purchased at stations and brought on board; some trains have food trolleys, but this is becoming less common, especially on shinkansen. Best, however, is the *ekiben,* a usually delightful form of the *bentō*, the traditional Japanese box lunch. Most regional stations have unique ekiben, featuring local specialties. Get one on from a platform vendor before boarding. It's Japanese cuisine at its finest and "funnest." Please note that eating and drinking on local buses, trains and subways is frowned upon.

Where does this train go?	*Kono densha wa doko yuki desu ka?*
Does this train stop at ~?	*Kono densha wa ~ ni tomarimasu ka?*
What is the next station?	*Tsugi no eki wa doko desu ka?*
The next stop is ~, isn't it?	*Tsugi wa ~ desu ne.*
Is ~ the next stop?	*Tsugi wa ~ desu ka?*
Where are we passing through now?	*Ima doko o hashitte imasu ka?*
What station is this?	*Koko wa doko no eki desu ka?*
Please tell me when we reach ~.	*~ ni tsuitara oshiete kudasai.*

When do we get to ~?	*~ ni wa itsu tsukimasu ka?*
How long will we stop here?	*Koko ni wa dono kurai tomarimasu ka?*
What time should I be back on board?	*Nan-ji made ni densha ni modotte konakereba narimasen ka?*
Where do I transfer for ~?	*~ e wa doko de norikaeru n'desu ka?*
May I sit here?	*Kono seki ni suwatte ii desu ka?*
I think this is my seat.	*Koko wa watashi no seki da to omoimasu ga.*
Can I smoke?	*Tabako o sutte mo ii desu ka?*

EXITING THE STATION

Getting out of most stations is quite easy. If you need to pay a fare adjustment, there will be a marked window at the exit for that purpose, or sometimes an automatic fare adjustment machine. Otherwise, you can hand the ticket to the member of station staff at the gate, who will calculate the difference for you (and call after you if you've tried to slip through without paying).

Is there a place to leave luggage for a few days?	*Ni san nichi nimotsu o azukatte kureru tokoro wa arimasu ka?*
How much is it to send my luggage to Shibuya?	*Shibuya ni onimitsu o okuritaindesuga, oikuradesu ka?*
baggage storage	*te-nimotsu ichi ji azukarijo*
I'd like to store my luggage.	*Nimotsu o azuketai n'desu ga.*
Which exit do I take for ~?	*~ wa dono deguchi ga ii desu ka?*
Where is the nearest ~?	*Ichiban chikai ~ wa doko desu ka?*
How long is it to the ~ by taxi	*~ made takushii de nan pun kurai desu ka?*
hotel	*hoteru*
business hotel	*bijinesu hoteru*
ryokan	*ryokan*
minshuku	*minshuku*
Is it far from here?	*Sore wa koko kara tōi desu ka?*

ESSENTIAL VERBS

to take a taxi *takushii ni noru*	to pay *harau*	to change, modify *henkō suru*
to take a train *densha ni noru*	to pay a fare adjustment *seisan suru*	cancel *torikesu*
to take a bus *basu ni noru*	to plan, expect *yotei suru*	to lose something *nakusu*

PROBLEMS AND REQUESTS

Problems on the train will be few: someone's sitting in your seat, you're sitting in someone else's seat, losing a ticket, or noisy children. If a polite request to a fellow passenger doesn't work or seems inappropriate, hunt down the conductor.

Be courteous to the conductor, for they can smooth out problems. The conductor is boss of the train. They usually don't speak much English, but they're patient with foreigners' queries and problems. If in need of the conductor and you can't wait for one to pass by, check the green car, which usually has its own conductors.

If you lose something or accidentally leave something on the train, go immediately to the station's Lost and Found, which should have signage in English. They can immediately find out which train you were on (if you provide them with the time you got off the train) and contact the station manager of other train stations. Lost items have a high percentage of being recovered in Japan.

Sorry, but I think this is a non-smoking car.	*Sumimasen ga koko wa kin'en-seki da to omoimasu ga.*
Your children are disturbing me.	*O-taku no o-ko-san ga chotto nigiyaka na n'desu ga.*
Your children are kicking my seat.	*O-taku no o-ko-san ga watashi no seki o kette iru n'desu ga.*
Can you be a little quieter?	*Mō sukoshi shizuka ni shite kuremasen ka?*
There's someone in my seat.	*Watashi no seki ni dareka ga suwatte imasu.*
Excuse me, but I think this is my seat.	*Sumimasen ga, kore wa watashi no seki da to omoimasu.*
Someone's smoking in the nonsmoking car.	*Kin'en-sha de tabako o sutte iru hito ga imasu.*
I'm confused and lost.	*Doko da ka sappari wakarimasen.*
I lost my ticket.	*Kippu o nakushimashita.*
I left my ~ on the train.	*Densha ni ~ o okiwasuremashita.*
I lost my ~.	*~ o nakushimashita.*
luggage	*nimotsu*
wallet	*saifu*
passport	*pasupōto*
money	*o-kane*
camera	*kamera*
coat	*kōto*
… and other things	*to hoka no mono*
What should I do?	*Dō sureba ii deshō ka?*
Please write a theft report.	*Tōnan shōmeisho o tsukutte kudasai.*
Can you let me off at ~?	*~ de oroshite moraemasu ka?*
Can I upgrade to first class?	*Guriin-sha e utsuremasu ka?*
Can I refund this ticket?	*Kono kippu o haraimodosemasu ka?*
Can I change my seat?	*Seki o utsutte mo ii desu ka?*

What station did you come from?	What seat were you in?
Doko no eki kara norimashita ka?	*Dono seki ni suwatte imashita ka?*

What train were you on?
Dono densha ni notte imashita ka?

I'll try to find someone who speaks English.
Dare ka Eigo o hanaseru hito o sagashitemimasu.

I'll contact the stations ahead to check for it.
Eki ni renraku shite shirabete moraimashou.

Where are you sitting?
Seki wa doko desu ka?

I'll try to take care of it.
Watashi ga nantoka shimashō.

Where are you getting off?
Doko de orimasu ka?

It can't be done right now.
Ima sugu ni wa dekimasen.

What size?
Ōkisa wa dore kurai desu ka?

What color?
Nani iro desu ka?

Please write down your name, telephone number, and address.
Kono kami ni, shimei, denwabangō, jūsho o kaite kudasai.

Yes, you can upgrade.
Gurīn-sha e utsuru koto ga dekimasu ka?

You can't upgrade now.
Ima wa guriin-sha ni wa utsuremasen.

I'll let you know later if it's possible.
Moshi daijōbu nara, atode o-shirase shimasu.

There is an extra charge for first class.
Yobun ni okane ga kakarimasu.

RENTING A CAR

Unless you are going to a very rural area, renting a car may not be the best idea. Streets are crowded and a challenge to navigate. If you do decide to rent a car, make sure that you have the proper documentation for a International Driving Permit to drive in Japan. This is valid for up to one year and can be obtained from your home country's automobile association, such as the AAA in the United States. It might also be a good idea to familiarize yourself with common Japanese road signs. You can find some of the main ones here: en.wikipedia.org/wiki/Road_signs_in_Japan

Toyota Rent a Car and Nippon Rent-A-Car are two big companies that have booths at airports as well as online reservation services.

PAYING HIGHWAY TOLLS

Japanese expressways charge tolls. Most rental cars come with a device called ETC, which will pay toll fees. At the end of the rental period, the rental company will charge you the amount that has accumulated on the ETC device.

TAKING A FERRY

An island country, Japan lends itself to water travel, and ferries connect major ports from Hokkaido to Okinawa. Ferries aren't cheap, and they're not especially elegant. On overnight trips there are usually two choices for sleeping: a semi-private cabin, or the second-class deck, with open, shared areas for sitting, sleeping, and eating. Although cheaper, second-class can be noisy until the wee hours and there is absolutely no privacy. As a foreigner and thus a curiosity, be prepared for stares but also, invitations for beer, sake, and a little English and Japanese language practice.

BOAT, SHIP	FERRY	PASSENGER SHIP	PIER	PORT/ HARBOR
fune	*ferii*	*kyakusen*	*sanbashi*	*minato*
CAPTAIN	STEWARD			
senchō	*suchuwādo*			

Where do I board the boat to ~?	*~ yuki no fune no noriba wa doko desu ka?*
What time do we board?	*Jōsen jikan wa nan-ji desu ka?*
What time does it depart?	*Itsu shukkō shimasu ka?*
Where is ~?	*~ wa doko desu ka?*
my berth	*watashi no shindai*
my cabin	*watashi no senshitsu*
the toilet	*toire*
the infirmary	*imushitsu*
the lifeboat	*kyūmei bōto*
a life jacket	*kyūmei dōi*
the pier	*sanbashi*
the port/harbor	*minato*
I'm quite seasick.	*Funayoi ga hidoi desu.*
Can you get a doctor?	*Isha o yonde moraemasu ka?*

Everyday Life and Practicalities

While cash is still widely used in Japan, payment for goods and services via debit or credit card, or via contactless payment such as Apple Pay is becoming the norm. Foreign tourists can also use a Welcome Suica or Pasmo Passport card (see page 63). You can withdraw cash at most Japanese ATMs, if you have authorized your card for overseas use with your home bank. Most convenience stores have ATMs, including 7-Eleven, Lawson and Family Mart.

Currency can easily be exchanged at the airport, at a Japanese bank, through a money changer such as World Currency Shop, or at your hotel. You will probably get the best rates at the bank. You may need to have your passport to exchange money, as well as the address of the place where you are staying. Japanese banks are usually quite busy, so it may be best to avoid peak times like lunch hour.

Before you leave your country, it may be useful to check out the fees associated with your debit and credit cards. Some cards without foreign transaction fees are the Venture Capital One card or the British Airways Visa Signature Card.

CHANGING MONEY

What's the exchange rate?	*Kawase rēto wa ikura desu ka?*
I'd like to change ~ dollars.	*~ doru o ryōgae shite kudasai.*
I'd like to change it to yen.	*En ni shitai n'desu ga.*
Give me large bills, please.	*Kōgaku shihei o kudasai.*
Give me small bills, please.	*Shōgaku shihei o kudasai.*
Can you change ~ to yen?	*~ o en ni kaete moraemasu ka?*
Change this to ~, please.	*~ ni kōkan shite kudasai.*

FOREIGN EXCHANGE *gaikoku kawase*	SINGAPORE $ *Shingapōru doru*	EURO *yūro*	CANADIAN $ *Kanada doru*

EXCHANGE RATE *kawase rēto*	HONG KONG $ *Honkon doru*	NEW ZEALAND $ *Nyū Jiirando doru*	AUSTRALIAN $ *Ōsutoraria doru*
US $ *doru*	BRITISH POUND *pondo*		

PUBLIC SIGNS AND NOTICES

SIGNS 掲示 *keiji*	ESCALATOR エスカレーター *esukarētā*	NO SMOKING 禁煙 *kin'en*	DO NOT USE 使用禁止 *shiyō kinshi*
CLOSED TODAY 本日休業 *honjitsu kyūgyō*	ELEVATOR エレベーター *erebētā*	RESERVED ご予約席 *kashikiri*	PROHIBITED 禁止 *~ kinshi*
CLOSED 準備中 *junbichū*	FOR SALE 売り物 *urimono*	GARBAGE CAN ゴミ箱 *gomibako*	KEEP OUT 立入禁止 *tachiiri kinshi*
OPEN 営業中 *eigyōchū*	DISCOUNT 割引 *waribiki*	OUT OF ORDER 故障中 *koshōchū*	NO TRESPASSING 侵入禁止 *shin'nyū kinshi*
OCCUPIED 使用中 *shiyōchū*	INFORMATION 案内 *an'nai*	WET PAINT ペンキ塗りたて *penki nuritate*	NO PHOTOS 撮影禁止 *satsuei kinshi*
EMERGENCY EXIT 非常口 *hijō guchi*	INFORMATION DESK 案内所 *a'naijo*	EMERGENCY BUTTON 非常呼出 *hijō yobidashi*	NO CROSSING 横断禁止 *ōdan kinshi*
ENTRANCE 入口 *iriguchi*	RECEPTION DESK 受付 *uketsuke*	WARNING 警告 *keikoku*	NO PARKING 駐車禁止 *chūsha kinshi*

EXIT	PULL	CAUTION	STOP
出口	引く	注意	止まれ
deguchi	*hiku*	*chūi*	*tomare*

AUTOMATIC DOORS	PUSH	DANGER	
自動ドア	押す	危険	
jidōdoa	*osu*	*kiken*	

LAUNDRY AND DRY CLEANING

There are dry-cleaning shops everywhere, most of them pick-up and drop-off outlets that send clothes to central cleaning centers. They are usually reasonably priced and do a great job. Coin laundries, or laundromats, are rarer but can be helpful if you are staying in Japan for a longer period of time.

Where is the nearest ~?	*Ichiban chikai ~ wa doko desu ka?*
laundry	*sentaku-ya*
dry cleaner	*dorai kuriiningu-ten*
laundromat	*koin randorii*
I have some laundry/dry cleaning.	*Sentaku/kuriiningu o tanomimasu.*
I'd like this pressed.	*Kore ni airon o kakete kudasai.*
I'd like this repaired.	*Kore o tsukurotte kudasai.*
Can you send it out?	*Dashite oite moraemasu ka?*
When will it be ready?	*Itsu dekimasu ka?*
Will it be ready by ~?	*~ made ni dekimasu ka?*
I need it ~.	*~ hitsuyō na n'desu ga.*
tonight	*konban*
tomorrow	*ashita*
the day after tomorrow	*asatte*
My laundry's been damaged.	*Sentakumono ga itande imashita.*
These clothes don't belong to me.	*Kore wa watashi no fuku de wa arimasen.*

SWEATER	SKIRT	SUIT	PANTS	LAUNDRY
sētā	*sukāto*	*sūtsu*	*zubon*	*sentaku-ya*

129

COAT	BLOUSE	NECKTIE	UNDERWEAR	DRY CLEANER
kōto	*burausu*	*nekutai*	*shitagi*	*dorai kuriiningu-ten*
DRESS	T-SHIRT	SHIRT	SOCKS	LAUNDROMAT
wanpiisu	*ti-shatsu*	*shatsu*	*kutsushita*	*koin randorii*

NATIONAL HOLIDAYS

1 January
New Year's Day
Ganjitsu

2nd Monday of January
Coming-of-Age Day
Seijin no hi

11 February
National Foundation Day
Kenkoku Kinen no hi

23 February
Emperor's Birthday
Ten'nō Tanjōbi

Around 20 March*
Vernal Equinox Day
Shunbun no hi

29 April
Showa Day
Shōwa no hi

3 May
Constitution Day
Kenpō Kinenbi

4 May
Greenery Day
Midori no hi

5 May
Children's Day
Kodomo no hi

3rd Monday of July
Marine Day
Umi no hi

11 August
Mountain Day
Yama no Hi

3rd Monday of September
Respect-for-Aged Day
Keirō no hi

Around 23 September*
Autumnal Equinox Day
Shūbun no hi

2nd Monday of October
Sports Day
Taiiku no hi

3 November
Culture Day
Bunka no hi

23 November
Labor Thanksgiving Day
Kinrō Kansha no hi

* Dates of the vernal and autumnal
equinoxes change from year to year.

TRAVEL SEASONS

There are a few weeks each year when seemingly the entire population of Japan is on vacation. Companies close down, subways are empty in the cities, and trains and highways leading from main urban areas are packed. They are: New Year's (*oshōgatsu*), from around 28 December to 4 January; Golden Week (*gōruden wiiku*), from 29 April to around 5 May; the *Obon* festival, from around 15 August for one or two weeks; and July and August, especially late August because of summer vacation.

New Year's is one of the biggest holidays in Japan. Here are some words associated with the New Year:

soba noodles eaten on New Year's Eve	*toshikoshi soba*
New Year's Eve	*hatsumōde*
special New Year's food	*osechi ryōri*
kite	*tako-age*
shrine	*jinja*
New Year's card	*nengajō*
money given by elders to children	*otoshidama*
New Year's TV singing competition	*kōhaku utagassen*

CINEMA AND OTHER VISUAL ENTERTAINMENT

The cinema and other forms of entertainment tend to be more expensive than in Europe or North America. Many Western-made movies are shown in their original language with Japanese subtitles, apart from blockbusters or kids' movies which are more likely to be dubbed into Japanese. For listings, check one of the English-language daily newspapers or the online magazine *Tokyo Journal* (tokyojournal.com).

I want to see ~.	*~ o mitai n'desu ga.*
I'd like to go see ~.	*~ o mi ni ikitai n'desu ga.*
Where can I see ~?	*~ wa doko de miraremasu ka?*
Should we go and see ~?	*Issho ni ~ o mi ni ikimasen ka?*
judo	*jūdō*
karate	*karate*
kendo	*kendō*
a baseball game	*yakyū/bēsubōru no shiai*
Kabuki	*kabuki*
Noh	*nō*
sumo	*sumō*
a concert	*ongakkai*
a movie	*eiga*
a drama/play	*engeki*
a play	*geki*
I'd like to try pachinko.	*Pachinko o yatte mitai desu.*

Where can one see Japanese flower arrangement?	*Ikebana o miru ni wa doko e ikeba ii desu ka?*
Where can one see a Japanese tea ceremony?	*Sadō o miru ni wa doko e ikeba ii desu ka?*
Do you know when it is?	*Sore wa itsu ka gozonji desu ka?*
What time does the ~ show begin?	*~ no kai wa nan-ji ni hajimarimasu ka*
first	*saisho*
last	*saigo*
What time does the show/performance begin?	*Kaien wa nan-ji desu ka?*
What time does the show/performance end?	*Shūen wa nan-ji desu ka?*
What time does the movie start?	*Eiga wa nan-ji kara desu ka?*
What time does the movie finish?	*Eiga wa nan-ji made desu ka?*
It finishes at (time).	*~ wa (jikan) made desu.*
It starts at (time).	*~ wa (jikan) kara desu.*
It's already started.	*Mō hajimatte imasu.*
Do you know where the ~ is?	*~ wa doko ka gozonji desu ka?*
movie theater	*eigakan*
concert hall	*konsāto hōru*
theater	*gekijō*
stage	*butai*
Is there an admission charge?	*Nyūjōryō wa irimasu ka?*
What is the admission charge?	*Nyūjōryō wa ikura desu ka?*
I'd like to reserve seats.	*Seki o yoyaku shitai n'desu ga.*
adult	*otona*
child	*kodomo*
advance ticket	*maeuriken*
entrance fee	*nyūjōryō*
reserved seating	*shitei-seki*
open/free seating	*jiyū-seki*
audience seat	*kyakuseki*
Please show me my seat.	*Seki ni an'nai shite kudasai.*

ACTOR	AUDIENCE	SUBTITLE	HORROR	SCIENCE FICTION
haiyū, *yakusha*	*kankyaku*	*jimaku*	*horā*	*esu-efu*
TRAGEDY	COMEDY	HISTORICAL	MYSTERY	
higeki	*kigeki*	*rekishimono*	*misuterii*	

MUSEUMS AND CONCERTS

I like to visit/go to ~.	*~ e iku no ga suki desu.*
art museums	*bijutsukan*
museums	*hakubutsukan*
displays, exhibitions	*tenrankai*
I like to look at ~.	*~ o miru no ga suki desu.*
I like to do ~.	*~ o suru no ga suki desu.*
I like listening to ~.	*~ o kiku no ga suki desu.*
I like playing ~ (piano, guitar).	*~ o hiku no ga suki desu.*
I like playing ~ (trumpet, flute).	*~ o fuku no ga suki desu.*

ART	CERAMICS	FOLK ART	PHOTOGRAPHY	ARTIST
geijutsu	*yakimono*	*mingei*	*shashin*	*geijutsuka*
CALLIGRAPHY	FINE ARTS	PAINTINGS	SCULPTURE	PAINTER
shodō	*bijutsu*	*e, kaiga*	*chōkoku*	*gaka*
MUSIC	CONCERT	SINGER	JAZZ	CLASSICAL MUSIC
ongaku	*konsāto*	*kashu*	*jazu*	*kurashikku*
INSTRUMENT	SONG	MUSICIAN	LATIN MUSIC	ROCK AND ROLL
gakki	*uta*	*ongakuka*	*raten ongaku*	*rokku*
PERFORMANCE	ORCHESTRA	FOLK SONGS	POPULAR MUSIC	KARAOKE
ensō	*ōkesutora*	*min'yō*	*poppusu*	*karaoke*

TOKYO ATTRACTIONS

Explore different areas in Tokyo to see various attractions. For example, Odaiba has a Madame Tussaud's wax museum, the Tokyo Joypolis game center and the Unko Museum which is dedicated to poop and toilet humor. Roppongi has plenty of museums, theaters and nightlife to keep you wowed for the entire time. Alternatively, you can find opera, ballet, dance and drama at the National Theater: ntj.jac.go.jp/en/theatre/national_theatre/.

Other popular tourist attractions include tours of the Imperial Palace; a stroll around the historic district of Asakusa that gives a feel of what Japan must have been like during the feudal era; or a vist to one of Tokyo's highest buildings to get a panoramic view of the city—these include Tokyo Tower, Tokyo Sky Tree, and the Tokyo City View observation deck on top of the Roppongi Hills building. There is also an observatory at the top of the Tokyo Metropolitan Government Building in Shinjuku.

INTERESTS AND ACTIVITIES

If you get into a conversation with a Japanese person, inevitably you'll be asked about your hobbies. To a Japanese person, "hobbies" means interests like skiing and golfing, not necessarily stamp or bug collecting.

What are your hobbies?	*Shumi wa nan desu ka?*
What do you like to do?	*Nani o suru no ga suki desu ka?*
I'm interested in ~.	*~ ni kyōmi ga arimasu.*
I love to ~.	*~ ga daisuki desu.*
I don't like ~.	*~ wa kirai desu.*
I want to study ~.	*~ o benkyō shitai desu.*
I'd like to try ~.	*~ o yatte mitai desu.*
I want to do ~.	*~ o shitai n'desu ga.*
I like to watch ~.	*~ o miru no ga suki desu.*
Would you like to ~?	*~ o shitai desu ka?*
I like ~.	*~ no ga suki desu.*
looking at architecture	*kenchiku o miru*
looking at art	*bijutsu o miru*
practising calligraphy	*shodō o suru*
playing cards	*toranpu o suru*
doing pottery	*yakimono o suru*
playing Japanese chess	*shōgi o suru*
dancing	*odori o suru*
watching Japanese movies	*Nihon no eiga o miru*
doing ikebana	*ikebana o suru*
looking at folk art	*mingei o miru*
playing games	*gēmu o suru*
visiting Japanese gardens	*Nihon teien o miru*
looking at Japanese art	*Nihon-ga o miru*
photography	*shashin o toru*
reading	*dokusho o suru*

making sculptures	*chōkoku o suru*
sightseeing	*kankō o suru*
traveling	*ryokō o suru*

ESSENTIAL VERBS

to appreciate, enjoy *kanshō suru*	to walk, stroll *sanpo suru*	to display, exhibit *tenji suru*
to be impressed *kandō suru*	to play an instrument *ensō suru*	to draw, paint *kaku*
to enjoy *tanoshimu*	to sing a song *uta o utau*	to sculpt *chōkoku suru*
to travel *ryokō suru*	to learn, to take lessons *narau*	to write, to publish *arawasu*

READING AND BOOKSHOPS

Who is your favorite ~?	*Suki-na ~ wa dare desu ka?*
author	*sakka*
novelist	*shōsetsuka*
poet	*shijin*
writer	*sakka*
I like to read ~.	*~ o yomu no ga suki desu.*

LITERATURE *bungaku*	ESSAYS *zuihitsu*	HISTORY *rekishi*	MYTHS *shinwa*	LEGENDS *densetsu*
BIOGRAPHIES *denki*	FAIRY TALES *dōwa*	HORROR *horā*	MYSTERIES *misuterii*	POETRY *shi*
CLASSICAL LITERATURE *koten bungaku*	GHOST STORIES *yūrei banashi*	MANGA *manga*	LOVE STORIES *ren'ai shōsetsu*	SCIENCE FICTION *esu-efu*

SPORTS

SPORTS	BOATING	HIKING	MOUNTAIN CLIMBING	SWIMMING
supōtsu	*bōto*	*haikingu*	*tozan*	*suiei*
AIKIDO	FISHING	HORSE-RIDING	SKATE-BOARDING	TABLE TENNIS
aikidō	*tsuri*	*jōba*	*sukebō*	*takkyū*
ARCHERY	AMERICAN FOOTBALL	JUDO	SKATING	TENNIS
kyūdō	*futtobōru*	*jūdō*	*sukēto*	*tenisu*
BASEBALL	GOLF	KARATE	SKIING	TRACK AND FIELD
yakyū	*gorufu*	*karate*	*sukii*	*rikujō kyōgi*
BASKETBALL	GYMNASTICS	KENDO	SOCCER	WATER SPORTS
basuketto bōru	*taisō*	*kendō*	*sakkā*	*suijō supōtsu*
BICYCLING	HANG GLIDING	MARATHON	SUMO	WIND SURFING
saikuringu	*hangu guraideingu*	*marason*	*sumō*	*uindosāfin*

ESSENTIAL VERBS

to take part in	to exercise	to win
sanka suru	*undō suru*	*katsu*
to compete	to practice, train	to lose
kyōsō suru	*keiko suru*	*makeru*

PHOTOGRAPHY

Photos are perhaps some of the most invaluable souvenirs when traveling to any country, including Japan.

Electronic stores like Bic Camera and Yodobashi Camera have great deals on cameras. Foreigners will also enjoy the luxury of not paying any tax for these items. Information can be found at the store and all you will need is your passport at the time of purchase.

Below are some useful phrases that can be used when asking someone to take a picture for you, or when shopping for a camera.

Can I take photos?	*Shashin o totte mo ii desu ka?*
Can I use the flash?	*Furasshu o tsukatte mo ii desu ka?*
Could you please take my photograph for me?	*Shashin o totte itadakemasu ka?*
Let's have our picture taken together.	*Issho ni shashin o totte kudasai.*
May I take your photograph?	*Shashin o torasete itadakemasu ka?*
A battery, please.	*Denchi o kudasai.*
This camera has a problem.	*Kamera no chōshi ga warui n'desu ga.*
Can you check it for me?	*Chotto mite moraemasu ka?*
Please fix my camera.	*Kamera o shūri shite kudasai.*

PHOTOGRAPH	NO PHOTOGRAPHS	NO FLASH
shashin	*satsuei kinshi*	*furasshu kinshi*
CAMERA	PHONE	ONE MORE PICTURE
kamera	*keitai*	*mō ichimai*

Seeing a Doctor

It's a hassle getting sick when traveling. But if you do, medical facilities are excellent in Japan, with high levels of care. However, Japan's health care establishment is rather conservative.

If consulting a Japanese doctor, you should know that Japan's medical tradition and system allow doctors to choose to tell you nothing about your diagnosis and treatment. The doctor need not say what's wrong, or give any explanation about the medicine prescribed. It is not unusual for a doctor to withhold information from a patient, if knowledge of a condition—terminal cancer is one example—might be upsetting.

Although Japan has a comprehensive national health care system, if you are a nonresident, you will be financially responsible for all treatment. However, the prices are much more reasonable than the United States and even if you don't have insurance, fees are not astronomical.

GETTING HELP

There are three options should you need a doctor. If you are staying at a first-class hotel, you can utilize the house physician at premium prices. Or, you can go to a public hospital or clinic, and be prepared for a long wait (two to three hours is not uncommon) and possible problems with language. Some travel insurance companies offer translation assistance. Otherwise, in major cities, you can go to one of the several private clinics staffed by English-speaking Western physicians. These hospitals can be searched on the Internet.

Call a doctor, please.	*Isha o yonde kudasai.*
Take me to the hospital.	*Byōin e tsurete itte kudasai.*
Do you know an English-speaking doctor?	*Eigo o hanaseru isha o shitte imasu ka?*
I need an interpreter.	*Tsūyaku ga hitsuyō desu.*

ESSENTIAL VERBS

to become sick *byōki ni naru*	to examine, to test *kensa suru*	to leave the hospital *taiin suru*
to be injured *kega o suru*	to take temperature *taion o hakaru*	to visit a patient *o-mimai ni iku*
to bleed *shukketsu suru*	to take an X-ray *rentogen o toru*	to be pregnant *ninshin shite iru*
to break a bone *kossetsu suru*	to give an injection *chūsha o suru*	to deliver a baby *shussan suru*
to sprain *nenza suru*	to operate *shujutsu suru*	to have an abortion *chūzetsu suru*
to get burned *yakedo suru*	to be hospitalized *nyūin suru*	to miscarry *ryūzan suru*

SYMPTOMS

It hurts here.	*Koko ga itamimasu.*
sharp pain	*kiri-kiri*
not sharp, but continuous	*shiku-shiku*
when you press hard	*tsuyoku osu to itamimasu*
when you press gently	*chotto oshita dake de tamimasu*
even when not touched	*nani mo shinakute mo itamimasu*
The pain comes and goes.	*Toki-doki itamimasu.*
I've had the pain since ~.	*~ kara itami ga arimasu.*
this morning	*kesa*
yesterday	*kinō*
the day before yesterday	*ototoi*
last week	*senshū*
I feel sick.	*Kibun ga warui desu.*
I feel nauseous.	*Hakike ga shimasu.*
I have a ~.	*~ o hikimashita.*
cold	*kaze*
chest cold	*seki no deru kaze*
head cold	*hana kaze*
I have a headache.	*Atama ga itai desu.*

I have a sharp pain.	*Kiri-kiri itamimasu.*
I have a throbbing pain.	*Zuki-zuki itamimasu.*
I've got a temperature.	*Netsu ga arimasu.*
I feel dizzy.	*Memai ga shimasu.*
I have a chill.	*Samuke ga shimasu.*
I have a cough.	*Seki ga demasu.*
I have a sore throat.	*Nodo ga itai desu.*
I have a stomachache.	*I ga itai desu.*
I've got diarrhea.	*Geri desu.*
I've been vomiting.	*Haite imasu.*
I'm constipated.	*Benpi desu.*
My chest hurts.	*Mune ga kurushii desu.*
I've got a toothache.	*Ha ga itai desu.*
I'm sleepy.	*Nemui desu.*
I'm tired.	*Tsukaremasu.*
I've got a poor appetite.	*Shokuyoku ga arimasen.*
Do I have to go to the hospital?	*Nyūin shinakereba ikemasen ka?*

SYMPTOMS *shōjō*	DIZZINESS *memai*	ITCHY *kayui*
CHILL *samuke*	FEVER *netsu*	LACK OF SLEEP *suimin busoku*
CONSTIPATION *benpi*	HANGOVER *futsukayoi*	NAUSEA *hakike*
COUGH *seki*	HEADACHE *zutsū*	PAIN *itami*
DIARRHEA *geri*	INDIGESTION *shokuatari*	HURTS *itai*

EXAMINATION

For Westerners used to frank discussions with their doctor, not to mention getting a second opinion when in doubt, the Japanese doctor's expectation of the patient's blind trust—and the aloofness of many doctors themselves—can be frustrating.

Where were you before Japan?
Nihon ni kuru mae wa doko ni imashitaka?

I want a ~ sample.
~kensa o shimasu.

Have you had this problem before?
Mae ni onaji shōjō ni natta koto ga arimasu ka?

blood
ketsueki, chi

What kinds of medicine are you taking?
Don'na kusuri o nonde imasu ka?

urine
nyō

I'll take your temperature.
Taion o hakarimasu.

stool
ben

I'll take your blood pressure.
Ketsuatsu o hakarimasu.

I'm going to take an X-ray.
Rentogen o torimasu.

HEALTH *kenkō*	CHECK UP *kenkō shindan*	TEST *kensa*	BLOOD *chi, ketsueki*	INJECTION *chūsha*
CONDITION *guai*	INITIAL EXAM *shoshin*	PULSE *taion*	BLOOD PRESSURE *ketsuatsu*	OPERATION *shujutsu*
TO EXAMINE *shinsatsu suru*	MEDICAL EXAM *shinsatsu*	BODY TEMPERATURE *myakuhaku*	BLOOD TYPE *ketsueki-gata*	EXAMINATION ROOM *shinsatsu shitsu*
GET SICK *byōki ni naru*	TREATMENT *teate*	URINE *nyō*	STOOL *ben*	VACCINATION *yobō chūsha*

THE BODY

BODY *karada*	FOREHEAD *hitai*	EYE *me*	CHEEK *hō*	TONGUE *shita*
HEAD *atama*	FACE *kao*	EYEBALL *medama*	NOSE *hana*	TOOTH *ha*
BRAIN *nō*	TEMPLE *komekami*	EYEBROW *mayuge*	MOUTH *kuchi*	JAW, CHIN *ago*
HAIR *kami no ke*	EAR *mimi*	EYELASH *matsuge*	LIP *kuchibiru*	NECK *kubi*
TORSO *dō*	SHOULDER *kata*	SIDE *yoko bara*	CHEST *mune*	HIP, WAIST *koshi*
RIB *rokkotsu*	ARMPIT *waki no shita*	BACK *senaka*	BELLY *o-naka*	BUTTOCKS *o-shiri*
INTERNAL *naizō*	MUSCLE *kin'niku*	ESOPHAGUS *shokudō*	LUNG *hai*	STOMACH *i, o-naka*
BLOOD *chi, ketsueki*	SKIN *hifu*	HEART *shinzō*	INTESTINES *chō*	GENITALS *seishokuki*
BONE *hone*	THROAT *nodo*	LIVER *kanzō*	KIDNEY *jinzō*	UTERUS *shikyū*
EXTREMITIES *te-ashi*	WRIST *te-kubi*	FINGERNAIL *tsume*	KNEE *hiza*	FOOT *ashi*
JOINT *kansetsu*	HAND *te*	FINGERPRINT *shimon*	SHIN *sune*	HEEL *kakato*
ARM *ude*	THUMB *oya yubi*	LEG *ashi*	CALF *fukurahagi*	TOE *tsumasaki*
ELBOW *hiji*	FINGER *yubi*	THIGH *futomomo*	ANKLE *ashi-kubi*	NERVE *shinkei*

PHYSICAL INJURIES

I fell and hit my ~.
My ~ hurts.
It hurts when I move it.

Koronde ~ o uchimashita.
~ ga itai desu.
Ugokasu to itamimasu.

BLEEDING *shukketsu*	BRUISE *uchimi*	CUT, GASH *kirikizu*	LUMP, BUMP *kobu*	SPRAIN *nenza*
BONE FRACTURE *kossetsu*	BURN *yakedo*	INTERNAL BLEEDING *naishukketsu*	SCRATCH *kasurikizu*	WOUND *kizu*

DIAGNOSIS

Although doctors in Japan have the right to not tell you what the diagnosis or treatment, many would understand because you are a foreigner that you want the entire picture. At most of the bigger hospitals, you can ask for an English translator to help you through the process and bridge the gap between Japan's traditions and your own cultural background.

I'm a diabetic.
I have an allergy to ~.

Watashi wa tōnyōbyō desu.
~ ni arerugii ga arimasu.

It's broken.
Orete imasu.

I'm giving you antibiotics.
Kōseibusshitsu o shohō shimasu.

It's sprained.
Nenza shite imasu.

You should go to the hospital for tests.
Kensa no tame ni byōin e itte kudasai.

It's infected.
Kanō shite imasu.

I want you to come back in ~ days.
~ nichikan tattara mata kite kudasai.

I believe that it's ~.
-da to omoimasu.

Are you allergic to any medlcines?
Kusuri no arerugii wa arimasu ka?

I think that you should go to the hospital for treatment.
Chiryō no tame ni byōin e itte kudasai.

ALLERGY	COMMON COLD	HEART ATTACK	MEASLES	PREGNANCY
arerugii	*futsū no kaze*	*shinzō hossa*	*hashika*	*ninshin*
APPENDICITIS	FATIGUE	HEPATITIS	MISCARRIAGE	RASH
mōchō	*tsukare*	*kanen*	*ryūzan*	*hosshin*
CANCER	FOOD POISONING	INFECTION	PNEUMONIA	URINARY INFECTION
gan	*shokuchūdoku*	*densen*	*haien*	*nyōdōen*
COLD, FLU	HAY FEVER	INFLUENZA	POISONING	
kaze	*kafunshō*	*infuruenza*	*chūdoku*	

MEDICINES

Japanese doctors often prescribe mountains of pills. Unfortunately, you may have no idea whether they are antibiotics or vitamins (the latter are commonly prescribed for illnesses). For minor ailments, there are over-the-counter medicines that can be bought at a pharmacy or drugstore.

Having your prescription filled is quite easy. Most can be filled at the hospital or clinic or you can find a pharmacist easily around town. Just look for the kanji 薬 or the hiragana くすり, both of which mean *kusuri* or "medicine." Many pharmacists can speak a little bit of English to help you with the appropriate dosage.

Please fill this prescription.	*Kono shohōsen de kusuri o kudasai.*
I need medicine for ~.	*~ no kusuri o kudasai.*
I'd like some ~.	*~ o kudasai.*

BEFORE MEALS	COLD	CONSTIPATION	FEVER	HEADACHE
shoku-zen	*kaze*	*benpi*	*netsu*	*zutsū*
AFTER MEALS	COUGH	DIARRHEA	HAY FEVER	UPSET STOMACH
shoku-go	*seki*	*geri*	*kafunshō*	*i no motare*

ANTIBIOTIC	HERBAL MEDICINE	DIARRHEA MEDICINE	HEADACHE MEDICINE	OINTMENT
kōseibusshitsu	*kanpōyaku*	*geri-dome*	*zutsūyaku*	*nankō*
ANTISEPTIC	COLD MEDICINE	EYE DROPS	LAXATIVE	SLEEPING PILL
shōdokuyaku	*kaze gusuri*	*me gusuri*	*gezai*	*suiminyaku*
ASPIRIN	COUGH MEDICINE	FEVER MEDICINE	PAIN-KILLER	STOMACH MEDICINE
asupirin	*seki-dome*	*genetsu-zai*	*itami-dome*	*igusuri*
PHARMACY	MEDICINE	PRESCRIPTION	PILL, TABLET	INTERNAL MEDICINE
yakkyoku	*kusuri*	*shohōsen*	*jōzai*	*nomigusuri*

REGISTERING AT THE HOSPITAL

Registering at the hospital is often quite easy and you will often find doctors who can speak some English. Because the paperwork might be a challenge, you can always ask at the entrance if there's anybody who can speak English. Since hospitals are often crowded, you may have to wait at the waiting area for a little while. If it's a true emergency though, you do get priority.

I'm going to send you to a specialist.
Senmon-i no tokoro e itte moraimasu.

Is there anybody who can speak English?
Dareka Eigo ga hanasemasu ka?

CARDI-OLOGY	GYNE-COLOGY	NEURO-SURGERY	ORTHOPE-DICS	UROLOGY
junkanki-ka	*fujin-ka*	*shinkei ge-ka*	*seikei ge-ka*	*hinyōki-ka*
DENTISTRY	INTERNAL MEDICINE	OBSTETRICS	PEDIATRICS	EAR/NOSE/ THROAT
shi-ka	*nai-ka*	*san-ka*	*shōni-ka*	*jibiinkō-ka*
DERMA-TOLOGY	NEUROLOGY	OPHTHAL-MOLOGY	RADIOLOGY	ANESTHESI-OLOGY
hifu-ka	*shinkei-ka*	*gan-ka*	*hōshasen-ka*	*masui-ka*
DOCTOR	AMBULANCE	HOSPITAL ROOM	PHARMACY	OUTPATIENT DEPT.
isha	*kyūkyūsha*	*byōshitsu*	*yakkyoku*	*gairai*
NURSE	CASHIER	RECEPTION DESK	MEDICAL COSTS	CONSULTING HOURS
kangoshi	*kaikei*	*uketsuke*	*iryōhi*	*shinryō jikan*
PATIENT	EMERGENCY ROOM	WAITING ROOM	WHEEL-CHAIR	VISITING HOURS
kanja	*kyūkyū byōin*	*machiai-shitsu*	*kuruma isu*	*menkai jikan*

AT THE HOSPITAL

I'm still not feeling well.	*Aikawarazu yoku arimasen.*
I feel a little better.	*Sukoshi yoku narimashita.*
I feel much better.	*Taihen yoku narimashita.*
Can I still travel?	*Ryokō o tsuzukete mo ii desu ka?*
How long do I have to take it easy?	*Nan nichi kurai ansei ga hitsuyō desu ka?*
How long until I get better?	*Dono kurai de yoku narimasu ka?*

CHAPTER 11

Police and Emergencies

Socially, male-dominated Japan may not be the modern woman's ideal place. On the street, though, Japan is nearly ideal, as crime rates are low and a woman can generally travel alone in most areas with little fear of attack or abuse. However, violent crime, while rare, does exist and women should exercise caution when walking alone at night. Some intoxicated Japanese males may become rude and sexually harass women on the street or on public transportation, and after dark it is always better to travel in groups and stick to well-lit streets with heavier foot traffic.

There is another uncomfortable, though not dangerous, place for a woman: the train. During rush hour, when trains are packed with people standing closely together, the groping of women (by perverts called *chikan*) is not unusual. Most subways and trains now have female-only cars operating during rush hour to help address this problem. These cars and their operating times are clearly marked on station platforms.

In cases when crimes are reported, police have considerable power, including detaining suspects for up to one month without charges. Like the *kōban* police boxes you see on street corners, police power (and the obedient behavior of citizens) is a residue of samurai times, when a wrong word or act could bring the unfavorable verdict of a swift sword.

In a low-crime place like Japan, the police spend most of their time patrolling neighborhoods on bicycles and giving directions.

EMERGENCIES

Help!	*Tasukete!*
I'm lost.	*Michi ni mayotte imasu.*
Please help me.	*Tasukete kudasai.*
Come with me.	*Issho ni kite kudasai.*
Where's the police box?	*Kōban wa doko desu ka?*
How do I get there?	*Dō yatte iku n'desu ka?*
Call the police, please.	*Keisatsu o yonde kudasai.*
Call a doctor, please.	*Isha o yonde kudasai.*

I must go to the hospital.	*Byōin e ikanakute wa narimasen.*
Please call an ambulance.	*Kyūkyūsha o yonde kudasai.*
Where is the lost and found?	*Ishitsubutsu toriatsukai-jo wa doko desu ka?*

AT THE POLICE STATION

If you've gone to the police with a problem, or if they've come to you with a problem, they may want to know a little more about you—see the questions below. Oblige. They are usually very fair and you can usually find a police officer who knows some English. Furthermore, they understand that you are scared and may struggle with the language.

Excuse me, what's written here?	*Sumimasen ga koko wa nanto kaite arimasu ka?*
Excuse me, could you write it in Roman letters?	*Sumimasen ga rōmaji de kaite kudasai.*
I need an interpreter.	*Tsūyaku ga hitsuyō desu.*
Does somebody here speak English?	*Dareka Eigo o hanaseru hito wa imasu ka?*

Do you have a passport?
Pasupōto wa arimasu ka?

Do you have money?
Okane wa arimasu ka?

Do you have an ID card?
Mibun shōmeisho wa arimasu ka?

How long are you staying in Japan?
Nihon ni wa donokurai iru tsumori desu ka?

Where are you from?

Please come with me to the police box.

Doko kara kimashitaka?

Issho ni kōban made kite kudasai.

LOST OR STOLEN

Excluding the danger presented by pickpockets who work places like airports, crowded trains, and busy shopping areas, money and belongings are relatively safe. A lost wallet or bag will usually turn up with all its contents intact. If you lose something on a train or subway, go to the Lost and Found office at the station. Tell them what you have lost, at around what time you boarded the train and which direction the train was headed. They will contact all likely train stations and if your lost property is found, they will have a person bring you the item. If the item cannot be located at that moment, you must fill out a lost and found form with your contact details.

If you lose something outside of the train and subway station, you can go to the nearest kōban police box. Again you will need to describe what you have lost and fill out a form.

Any traveler should always have photocopies of their passport, visa, and other important papers. Likewise, serial numbers are invaluable in retrieving lost or—rarely—stolen items like cameras and laptop computers. Keeping a card from your hotel in your bag will aid in getting the bag back to you, should you lose it. If you require a police report in order to be reimbursed by your insurance company for lost or stolen items, you should be aware that it will be difficult to get one outside of the major cities. In any case, it'll be in Japanese. It will be the luck of the draw whether the person is proficient in both English and Japanese. Your travel insurance provider should be able to assist you through the process.

I lost ~.	*~ o nakushimashita.*
I left ~ in a taxi/train/bus.	*takushii/densha/basu ni ~ o wasuremashita.*
My ~ was stolen.	*~ o nusumaremashita.*
wallet	*saifu*
cash	*genkin*
passport	*pasupōto*
driver's license	*menkyoshō*
ID card	*mibun shōmeisho*
camera	*kamera*
glasses	*megane*
handbag	*handobaggu*
package/ luggage	*nimotsu*
suitcase	*sūtsukēsu*
watch	*tokei*
laptop	*rapputoppu*
tablet	*taburetto*
smartphone	*sumaho*

Please write down your name, telephone number, and address in Japan.
Koko ni namae, denwa bangō, jūsho o kaite kudasai.

Please describe the item(s).
Dōiu mono desu ka?

PROBLEMS

There's/It's a/an ~.	*~ desu.*
fire	*kaji*
accident	*jiko*
traffic accident	*kōtsū jiko*
crime	*hanzai*
theft	*nusumi*
fraud, scam	*sagi*
pickpocket	*suri*
thief	*dorobō*
Whom should I tell?	*Dare ni shirasetara ii desu ka?*

FIRE	ROAD ACCIDENT	CRIME	FRAUD, SCAM	DETECTIVE
kaji	*kōtsū jiko*	*hanzai*	*sagi*	*keiji*
FIRE TRUCK	AMBULANCE	THEFT	POLICE	POLICE STATION
shōbōsha	*kyūkyūsha*	*nusumi*	*keisatsu*	*keisatsusho*
FIRE STATION	INJURY	PICKPOCKET	POLICE OFFICER	POLICE BOX
shōbōsho	*kega*	*suri*	*keisatsukan*	*kōban*
NATIONALITY	JUDGE	CRIMINAL	OFFENSE	EVIDENCE
kokuseki	*saibankan*	*han'nin*	*hankō*	*shōko*
EMBASSY	LAWYER	THIEF	GUILT	PRISON, JAIL
taishikan	*bengoshi*	*dorobō*	*yūzai*	*keimusho*
COURT OF LAW	WITNESS	LEGAL ADVICE	INNOCENCE	INSURANCE
saibansho	*shōnin*	*hōritsu sōdan*	*muzai*	*hoken*

English-Japanese

ENGLISH	ROMAJI	JAPANESE

A

a little	*chotto*	ちょっと
absolutely	*zettai ni*	絶対に
accommodation	*shukuhaku*	宿泊
address	*jūsho*	住所
adult	*otona*	大人
again	*mata*	また
airplane	*hikōki*	飛行機
airport	*kūkō*	空港
aisle	*tsūro*	通路
all	*zenbu*	全部
all right	*daijōbu*	大丈夫
allergies	*arerugii*	アレルギー
always	*itsumo*	いつも
a.m.	*gozen*	午前
ambulance	*kyūkyūsha*	救急車
America	*Amerika*	アメリカ
American football	*Amefuto*	アメフト
amusement park	*yūenchi*	遊園地
angry, to be	*okoru*	怒る
app	*apuri*	アプリ
apple	*ringo*	りんご
Arabic language	*Arabiago*	アラビア語
aroma	*kaori*	香り
arrival	*tōchaku*	到着
art	*bijutsu*	美術
Asia	*Ajia*	アジア
aunt	*obasan*	おばさん
autumn, fall	*aki*	秋

B

bad	*warui*	悪い
baggage	*te-nimotsu*	手荷物

ENGLISH	ROMAJI	JAPANESE
banana	*banana*	バナナ
bank	*ginkō*	銀行
bar	*izakaya*	居酒屋
bargain	*o-kaidokuhin*	お買い得品
bath	*o-furo*	お風呂
baseball	*yakyū*	野球
basketball	*basukettobōru*	バスケットボール
bathroom	*o-tearai*	お手洗い
battery	*denchi*	電池
beef	*gyūniku*	牛肉
bird	*tori*	鳥
black	*kuro*	黒
black pepper	*koshō*	こしょう
blood	*chi*	ち
blowfish	*fugu*	ふぐ
blue	*ao*	青
boat	*fune*	船
book	*hon*	本
bookstore	*hon-ya*	本屋
borrow, to	*kariru*	借りる
both	*ryōhō*	両方
boyfriend	*kareshi*	彼氏
bread	*pan*	パン
breakfast	*asa gohan*	朝ご飯
bridge	*hashi*	橋
bright	*akarui*	明るい
Britain	*Igirisu*	イギリス
brown	*chairo*	茶色
Buddhism	*Bukkyō*	仏教
budget	*yosan*	予算
building	*tatemono*	建物
bullet train	*shinkansen*	新幹線
bus	*basu*	バス
business card	*meishi*	名刺
busy	*isogashii*	忙しい
buy, to	*kau*	買う

ENGLISH	ROMAJI	JAPANESE

C

Canada	*Kanada*	カナダ
car	*kuruma*	車
carrot	*ninjin*	にんじん
cash	*genkin*	現金
cash register	*reji*	レジ
castle	*o-shiro*	お城
cat	*neko*	猫
caution	*chūi*	注意
center	*chūshin*	中心
chair	*isu*	いす
change (*money returned*)	*otsuri*	おつり
charger	*jūdenki*	じゅうでんき
check (*restaurant bill*)	*okanjō*	お勘定
chef	*shefu*	シェフ
cherry blossoms	*sakura*	さくら
chicken (*food*)	*chikin*	チキン
child/children	*kodomo*	子供
China	*Chūgoku*	中国
Chinese citizen	*Chūgoku-jin*	中国人
Chinese language	*Chūgokugo*	中国語
chocolate	*chokorēto*	チョコレート
chopsticks	*o-hashi*	お箸
Christian	*Kirisuto-kyō*	キリスト教
church	*kyōkai*	教会
city	*shi*	市
clean	*kirei*	きれい
climate	*kikō*	気候
climb, to	*noboru*	登る
clock	*tokei*	時計
close, to	*shimeru*	閉める
clothes	*fuku*	服
cloud	*kumo*	雲
coat	*kōto*	コート
coffee	*kōhii*	コーヒー
coffee shop	*kissaten*	喫茶店
coin	*kozeni*	小銭
cold	*samui*	寒い

155

ENGLISH	ROMAJI	JAPANESE
a cold (*illness*)	*kaze*	かぜ
college	*daigaku*	大学
color	*iro*	色
company	*kaisha*	会社
computer	*pasokon*	パソコン
concert	*konsāto*	コンサート
condominium	*manshon*	マンション
continue, to	*tsudukeru*	続ける
contract	*keiyaku*	契約
convenience store	*konbini*	コンビニ
cook, to	*ryōri suru*	料理する
cookbook	*ryōri no hon*	料理の本
correct	*tadashii*	正しい
cough	*seki*	せき
country	*kuni*	国
cousin	*itoko*	いとこ
COVID	*korona*	コロナ
crab	*kani*	かに
cram school	*juku*	塾
crowded	*konde iru*	混んでいる
cry	*naku*	泣く
culture	*bunka*	文化
customer	*o-kyaku*	お客
cute	*kawaii*	かわいい

D

danger	*kiken*	危険
dark	*kurai*	くらい
daughter	*musume*	娘
day	*hi*	日
day off, holiday	*kyūjitsu*	休日
decide, to	*kimeru*	決める
delay, to	*okureru*	遅れる
delicious	*oishii*	美味しい
deliver, to	*haitatsu suru*	配達する
dentist	*haisha*	歯医者
depart, to	*shuppatsu suru*	出発する
department store	*depāto*	デパート

ENGLISH	ROMAJI	JAPANESE
departure	*shuppatsu*	出発
desk	*tsukue*	つくえ
detergent	*senzai*	洗剤
diarrhea	*geri*	下痢
dictionary	*jisho*	辞書
die, to	*shinu*	死ぬ
difficult	*muzukashii*	難しい
dinner	*ban gohan*	晩御飯
disagree, to	*hantai suru*	反対する
discount	*waribiki*	割引
dish; plate	*sara*	皿
distance	*kyori*	距離
doctor	*oisha-san*	お医者さん
document	*shorui*	書類
dog	*inu*	犬
domestic	*kokunai*	国内
door	*doa*	ドア
dorm	*ryō*	りょう
dream	*yume*	夢
drink, to	*nomu*	飲む
drinks	*nomimono*	飲み物
drive, to	*unten suru*	運転する
driver's license	*unten menkyosho*	運転免許証
dry	*kawaita*	乾いた
duty-free item	*menzeihin*	免税品

E

ear	*mimi*	耳
early	*hayaku*	早く
earth	*chikyū*	地球
east	*higashi*	東
eat, to	*taberu*	食べる
economy	*keizai*	経済
education	*kyōiku*	教育
eel	*unagi*	うなぎ
egg	*tamago*	たまご
eggplant	*nasu*	なす
Egypt	*Ejiputo*	エジプト

ENGLISH	ROMAJI	JAPANESE
elbow	*hiji*	ひじ
election	*senkyo*	選挙
electric	*denki*	電気
elevator	*erabētā*	エレベーター
embassy	*taishikan*	大使館
empty	*kara*	空
end	*owari*	終わり
English	*Eigo*	英語
entrance (*to house*)	*genkan*	玄関
entrance (*general*)	*iriguchi*	入り口
envelope	*fūtō*	封筒
eraser	*keshigomu*	消しゴム
escalator	*esukarētā*	エスカレーター
Europe	*Yōroppa*	ヨーロッパ
evening	*yūgata*	夕方
exam	*shiken*	試験
exchange	*kōkan*	交換
exercise	*undō*	運動
exit	*deguchi*	出口
expensive	*takai*	高い
eye	*me*	目

F

face	*kao*	顔
factory	*kōjō*	工場
famous	*yūmei*	有名
far	*tōi*	遠い
fare (*for transport*)	*unchin*	運賃
father	*otōsan*	お父さん
favor	*onegai*	お願い
female	*josei*	女性
final	*saigo*	最後
find, to	*sagasu*	探す
fire	*hi*	火
first	*saisho*	最初
fish	*sakana*	魚
fishing	*tsuri*	釣り
flag	*hata*	はた

ENGLISH	ROMAJI	JAPANESE
floor	*kai*	階
florist	*hana-ya*	花屋
flower	*hana*	花
flu	*infuruenza*	インフルエンザ
fog	*kiri*	きり
food	*tabemono*	食べ物
foot	*ashi*	足
football, American	*Amefuto*	アメフト
foreign country	*gaikoku*	外国
fork	*fōku*	フォーク
fragile	*waremono*	割れ物
fragrance	*kaori*	香り
free (*unoccupied*)	*tada*	ただ
freedom	*jiyū*	自由
freezer	*reitōkō*	冷凍庫
fresh	*shinsen*	新鮮
Friday	*Kin-yōbi*	金曜日
fridge	*reizōkō*	冷蔵庫
friend	*tomodachi*	友達
frog	*kaeru*	かえる
front desk	*furonto*	フロント
full	*ippai*	いっぱい

G

game	*gēmu*	ゲーム
garage	*garēji*	ガレージ
garbage	*gomi*	ゴミ
garden	*ni wa*	庭
gasoline	*gasorin*	ガソリン
gate	*mon*	門
girl	*on'na no ko*	女の子
girlfriend	*kanojo*	彼女
glasses	*megane*	メガネ
glove	*tebukuro*	手袋
glue	*nori*	のり
GPS (*car navigation*)	*nabi*	ナビ
go, to	*iku*	行く
go out, to	*dekakeru*	出かける

ENGLISH	ROMAJI	JAPANESE
goal	*gōru*	ゴール
god	*kami*	神
gold	*kin*	金
golf	*gorufu*	ゴルフ
good	*ii*	良い
goodbye	*sayōnara*	さようなら
graduation	*sotsugyōshiki*	卒業式
grammar	*bunpō*	文法
grass	*kusa*	草
green	*midori*	緑
green tea; tea	*o-cha*	お茶
greeting	*aisatsu*	あいさつ
guide	*an'nai*	案内
gum	*gamu*	ガム

H

hair	*kami*	髪
ham	*hamu*	ハム
hamburger	*hanbāgā*	ハンバーガー
hand	*te*	手
handkerchief	*hankachi*	ハンカチ
happy	*shiawase*	幸せ
Happy Birthday	*Otanjōbi Omedetō*	お誕生日おめでとう
hat	*bōshi*	帽子
head	*atama*	頭
headache	*zutsū*	頭痛
health	*kenkō*	健康
heart	*shinzō*	心臓
heater	*danbōki*	暖房器
heavy	*omoi*	おもい
height	*takasa*	高さ
helicopter	*heri*	ヘリ
help	*tasukete*	助けて
herb	*hābu*	ハーブ
hiking	*haikingu*	ハイキング
history	*rekishi*	歴史
hockey	*hokkē*	ホッケー
holiday, day off	*kyūjitsu*	休日

ENGLISH	ROMAJI	JAPANESE
home	*katei*	家庭
horse	*uma*	馬
hospital	*byōin*	病院
hot	*atsui*	暑い
hot water	*o-yu*	お湯
hotel	*hoteru*	ホテル
house	*uchi*	うち
how much	*ikura*	いくら
hungry	*onaka ga suita*	おなかがすいた
hurry, in a	*isogu*	急ぐ
husband	*otto*	夫

I

ice	*kōri*	氷
illegal	*fuhō*	不法
illness	*byōki*	病気
income	*shūnyū*	収入
India	*Indo*	インド
inexpensive	*yasui*	安い
injection	*chūsha*	ちゅうしゃ
insect	*mushi*	虫
inside	*naka*	中
insurance	*hoken*	保険
Internet	*Intānetto*	インターネット
iron	*airon*	アイロン
Israel	*Isuraeru*	イスラエル
itch	*kayumi*	かゆみ

J

jacket	*jaketto*	ジャケット
Japan	*Nihon*	日本
Japanese cuisine	*Nihon-shoku*	日本食
Japanese language	*Nihongo*	日本語
jet lag	*jisaboke*	時差ボケ
job	*shigoto*	仕事
joke	*jōdan*	冗談

ENGLISH	ROMAJI	JAPANESE

K

ketchup	*kechappu*	ケチャップ
key	*kagi*	鍵
kilo	*kiro*	キロ
kiss	*kisu*	キス
kitchen	*daidokoro*	台所
knee	*hiza*	膝
knife	*naifu*	ナイフ
knit, to	*amu*	編む
Korea	*Kankoku*	韓国
Korean citizen	*Kankoku-jin*	韓国人
Korean language	*Kankokugo*	韓国語

L

ladder	*hashigo*	はしご
lake	*mizu'umi*	湖
last	*saigo*	最後
late	*osoi*	遅い
laugh	*warau*	笑う
laundry	*sentaku*	せんたく
lawyer	*bengoshi*	弁護士
left (*direction*)	*hidari*	左
lemon	*remon*	レモン
letter	*tegami*	手紙
library	*toshokan*	図書館
a lie	*uso*	うそ
light (*vs. dark*)	*akarui*	明るい
lights	*denki*	電気
lip	*kuchibiru*	唇
liquid	*ekitai*	液体
little	*chiisai*	小さい
lobby	*robii*	ロビー
locker	*rokkā*	ロッカー
(*I am*) lost	*mayotte imasu*	迷っています
lost it (*an item*)	*nakushimashita*	なくしました
lost item	*wasuremono*	忘れ物
lunch	*o-hiru gohan*	お昼ご飯

ENGLISH	ROMAJI	JAPANESE

M

magazine	*zasshi*	ざっし
mail	*yūbin*	郵便
male	*dansei*	男性
many	*takusan*	たくさん
map	*chizu*	地図
marry, to	*kekkon suru*	結婚する
math	*sūgaku*	数学
meal	*shokuji*	食事
meat	*niku*	肉
medicine	*kusuri*	薬
meet, to	*au*	会う
menu	*menyū*	メニュー
middle	*man'naka*	真ん中
mine	*watashi no*	私の
mirror	*kagami*	鏡
mistake	*machigae*	間違え
Monday	*Getsu-yōbi*	月曜日
money	*okane*	お金
mother	*okāsan*	お母さん
more	*motto*	もっと
morning	*asa*	朝
mountain	*yama*	山
mouse	*nezumi*	ねずみ
mouth	*kuchi*	口
movie	*eiga*	映画
movie theater	*eigakan*	映画館
music	*ongaku*	音楽

N

name	*namae*	名前
nap	*hirune*	昼寝
napkin	*napukin*	ナプキン
nationality	*kokuseki*	国籍
nature	*shizen*	自然
nausea	*hakike*	吐き気
near	*chikai*	近い
necessary	*hitsuyō*	必要

ENGLISH	ROMAJI	JAPANESE
Netherlands	*Oranda*	オランダ
new	*atarashii*	新しい
news	*nyūsu*	ニュース
newspaper	*shinbun*	新聞
New Year	*Shin'nen*	新年
next	*tsugi*	次
night	*yoru*	夜
no	*iie*	いいえ
noodles	*men*	めん
noisy	*urusai*	うるさい
nonsmoking	*kinen*	禁煙
north	*kita*	北
normal	*futsū*	普通
nose	*hana*	鼻
now	*ima*	今
number	*kazu*	数
nurse	*kangoshi*	看護師

O

occasion	*bāi*	場合
ocean	*umi*	海
office	*jimosho*	事務所
oil	*abura*	油
old (*vs. new*)	*furui*	古い
only	*dake*	だけ
open	*akeru*	開ける
orange	*orenji*	オレンジ
to order	*chūmon*	注文
order (*sequence*)	*junban*	順番
outside	*soto*	外
oven	*ōbun*	オーブン
oxygen	*sanso*	酸素
oyster	*kaki*	かき

P

Pacific Ocean	*Taiheiyō*	太平洋
page	*pēji*	ページ
painful	*itai*	いたい

ENGLISH	ROMAJI	JAPANESE
paint	*penki*	ペンキ
painting	*e*	絵
pajamas	*pajama*	パジャマ
pancake	*hottokēki*	ホットケーキ
pants	*zubon*	ズボン
paper	*kami*	紙
parent	*oya*	親
park	*kōen*	公園
parking	*chūsha*	駐車
part-time job	*arubaito*	アルバイト
passport	*pasupōto*	パスポート
part	*bubun*	部分
patient (*sick person*)	*kanja*	患者
pay, to	*harau*	払う
peace	*heiwa*	平和
pear	*nashi*	なし
pen	*pen*	ペン
pencil	*enpitsu*	鉛筆
perfect	*kanpeki*	完ぺき
person	*hito*	人
phone	*denwa*	電話
phone (*mobile*)	*keitai*	携帯
photo	*shashin*	写真
pickpocket	*suri*	スリ
plan	*keikaku*	計画
play, to	*asobu*	遊ぶ
poem	*shi*	詩
poison	*doku*	毒
police	*keikan*	警官
police box	*kōban*	交番
politician	*seijika*	政治家
population	*jinkō*	人口
pork	*butaniku*	豚肉
p.m.	*gogo*	午後
Portugal	*Porutogaru*	ポルトガル
possible	*kanō*	可能
postcard	*hagaki*	ハガキ
postcode	*yūbin bangō*	郵便番号

ENGLISH	ROMAJI	JAPANESE
post office	*yūbin kyoku*	郵便局
potato	*jagaimo*	ジャガイモ
pound	*pondo*	ポンド
power	*chikara*	力
practice	*renshū*	練習
pray, to	*inoru*	祈る
prefecture	*ken*	県
pregnant	*ninshin*	妊娠
president	*daitōryō*	大統領
pretty	*kirei*	きれい
price	*nedan*	値段
problem	*mondai*	問題
promise	*yakusoku*	やくそく
purple	*murasaki*	紫
purpose	*mokuteki*	目的
push, to	*osu*	押す

Q

quick	*hayai*	早い
quiet	*shizuka*	静か
quit, to	*yameru*	やめる

R

rabbit	*usagi*	うさぎ
rain	*ame*	雨
raw	*nama*	生
read, to	*yomu*	読む
rear	*ushiro*	後ろ
receipt	*ryōshūsho*	領収書
red	*aka*	赤
religion	*shūkyō*	宗教
remember, to	*omoidasu*	思い出す
repair	*shūri*	修理
repeat, to	*kurikaesu*	繰り返す
reply	*henji*	返事
reserve, to	*yoyaku suru*	予約する
respect	*sonkei*	尊敬
retire	*taishoku*	退職

ENGLISH	ROMAJI	JAPANESE
rice (*cooked*)	*gohan*	ご飯
rice (*uncooked*)	*kome*	米
rich	*kanemochi*	金持ち
right (*direction*)	*migi*	右
river	*kawa*	川
road	*michi*	道
robbery	*gōtō*	強盗
roof	*yane*	屋根
room	*heya*	部屋
rose	*bara*	バラ
rude	*shitsurei*	失礼
rule	*kisoku*	きそく
rumor	*uwasa*	うわさ
run, to	*hashiru*	走る
Russia	*Roshia*	ロシア

S

sad	*kanashii*	悲しい
safe	*anzen*	安全
salary	*kyūryō*	給料
salt	*shio*	塩
same	*onaji*	同じ
sand	*suna*	砂
sandwich	*sandoitchi*	サンドイッチ
Saturday	*Do-yōbi*	土曜日
scary	*kowai*	こわい
schedule	*yotei*	予定
school	*gakkō*	学校
science	*kagaku*	科学
sea	*umi*	海
season	*kisetsu*	季節
seat	*seki*	席
second helping	*okawari*	おかわり
set menu	*tēshoku*	定食
shirt	*shatsu*	シャツ
shoes	*kutsu*	靴
shopping	*kaimono*	買い物
shoulder	*kata*	かた

ENGLISH	ROMAJI	JAPANESE
to show around	*an'nai*	案内
shower	*shawā*	シャワー
silver	*gin*	銀
sing, to	*utau*	歌う
size	*saizu*	サイズ
ski	*sukii*	スキー
sleep, to	*neru*	寝る
sleepy	*nemui*	眠い
slow	*osoi*	遅い
smartphone	*sumaho*	スマホ
snow	*yuki*	雪
soap	*sekken*	石鹸
soccer	*sakkā*	サッカー
social media	*SNS*	エスエヌエス
sock	*kutsushita*	靴下
sold out	*urikire*	売り切れ
son	*musuko*	息子
sound	*oto*	音
souvenirs	*omiyage*	お土産
soy sauce	*shōyu*	醤油
speak, to	*hanasu*	話す
speed	*hayasa*	速さ
spirit	*kokoro*	心
spring	*haru*	春
squid	*ika*	イカ
stairs	*kaidan*	階段
stamp	*kitte*	切手
stand, to	*tatsu*	立つ
start, to	*hajimeru*	始める
stomach	*o-naka*	おなか
store	*mise*	店
story, tale	*monogatari*	物語
straight ahead	*massugu*	まっすぐ
strawberry	*ichigo*	いちご
strong	*tsuyoi*	強い
study	*benkyō*	勉強
subway	*chikatetsu*	地下鉄
summer	*natsu*	夏

ENGLISH	ROMAJI	JAPANESE
Sunday	*Nichi-yōbi*	日曜日
sunny	*hare*	晴
sweat	*ase*	汗
sweet	*amai*	甘い
swim, to	*oyogu*	泳ぐ

T

story, tale	*monogatari*	物語
taxi	*takushii*	タクシー
tea; green tea	*o-cha*	お茶
television	*terebi*	テレビ
thank you	*arigatō gozaimasu*	ありがとうございます
thankful	*kansha*	感謝
thirsty	*nodo ga kawaita*	のどがかわいた
Thursday	*Moku-yōbi*	木曜日
ticket	*kippu*	切符
time	*jikan*	時間
tired	*tsukarete iru*	疲れている
today	*kyō*	今日
tour	*tsuā*	ツアー
toy	*omocha*	おもちゃ
traditional	*dentō*	伝統
train	*densha*	電車
train station	*eki*	駅
tree	*ki*	木
Tuesday	*Ka-yōbi*	火曜日

U

umbrella	*kasa*	傘
unappetizing	*mazui*	まずい
under	*shita*	下
until	*made*	まで
useful	*benri*	便利

V

vacuum	*sōjiki*	掃除機
vegetables	*yasai*	野菜
vending machine	*jihan-ki*	自販機

ENGLISH	ROMAJI	JAPANESE
village	*mura*	村
volcano	*kazan*	火山

W

walk, to	*aruku*	歩く
water	*o-mizu*	お水
waterfall	*taki*	滝
weather	*o-tenki*	お天気
Wednesday	*Sui-yobi*	水曜日
weekday	*heijitsu*	平日
west	*nishi*	西
what	*nani*	何
when	*itsu*	いつ
where	*doko*	どこ
white	*shiro*	白
who	*dare*	だれ
why	*naze*	なぜ
wind	*kaze*	風
window	*mado*	窓
winter	*fuyu*	冬

Y

yellow	*kiiro*	きいろ
yesterday	*kinō*	昨日
yet	*mada*	まだ
you	*anata*	あなた
young	*wakai*	若い

Z

zoo	*dōbutsuen*	動物園

Japanese-English

ROMAJI	JAPANESE	ENGLISH

A

abura	油	oil
au	会う	to meet
airon	アイロン	iron
aisatsu	あいさつ	greeting
Ajia	アジア	Asia
aka	赤	red
akarui	明るい	bright, light (*vs. dark*)
akeru	開ける	open
aki	秋	autumn, fall
amai	甘い	sweet
amari	あまり	not very
ame	雨	rain
ame	飴	candy
Amefuto	アメフト	American football
Amerika	アメリカ	America
Amerika-jin	アメリカ人	US citizen
amu	編む	to knit
anata	あなた	you
an'nai suru	案内する	to guide, to show around
ano	あの	that [noun] over there
anō	あのう	let me see…
anzen	安全	safe
ao	青	blue
apuri	アプリ	app
Arabiago	アラビア語	Arabic language
are	あれ	that over there
arerugii	アレルギー	allergies
arigatō gozaimasu	ありがとうございます	thank you
arubaito	アルバイト	part-time job
aruku	歩く	to walk
asa	朝	morning
asa gohan	朝ご飯	breakfast

ROMAJI	JAPANESE	ENGLISH
asatte	あさって	the day after tomorrow
ase	汗	sweat
ashi	足	foot
ashita	明日	tomorrow
asobu	遊ぶ	to play
asoko	あそこ	over there
atama	頭	head
atarashii	新しい	new
atsui	暑い	hot

B

bāi	場合	occasion
baiten	売店	kiosk
ban	晩	evening
banana	バナナ	banana
ban gohan	晩御飯	dinner
bara	バラ	rose
barēbōru	バレーボール	volleyball
basu	バス	bus
basukettobōru	バスケットボール	basketball
beddo	ベッド	bed
bengoshi	弁護士	lawyer
benkyō suru	勉強する	to study
benri	便利	useful
bentō	弁当	box lunch
bijutsu	美術	art
boku	僕	I (*used by males*)
bōshi	帽子	hat
bubun	部分	part
bukkyō	仏教	Buddhism
bunka	文化	culture
bunpō	文法	grammar
buta	豚	pig
butaniku	豚肉	pork
byōin	病院	hospital
byōki	病気	illness

ROMAJI	JAPANESE	ENGLISH

C

chairo	茶色	brown
chi	ち	blood
chiisai	小さい	little
chikai	近い	near
chikara	力	power
chikatetsu	地下鉄	subway
chikin	チキン	chicken (*food*)
chikyū	地球	earth
chizu	地図	map
chokorēto	チョコレート	chocolate
chotto	ちょっと	a little
Chūgoku	中国	China
Chūgokugo	中国語	Chinese language
Chūgoku-jin	中国人	Chinese citizen
chūi	注意	caution
chūmon suru	注文する	to order
chūsha	ちゅうしゃ	injection
chūsha	駐車	parking
chūshin	中心	center

D

daidokoro	台所	kitchen
daigaku	大学	college
daigakusei	大学生	college student
daiji	大事	important
daijōbu	大丈夫	all right
daisuki	大好き	(*I*) love (*something*)
daitōryō	大統領	president
dake	だけ	only
dame	だめ	not good
danbōki	暖房器	heater
dansei	男性	male
dare	だれ	who
deguchi	出口	exit
dekakeru	出かける	to go out
demo	でも	but
denchi	電池	battery

ROMAJI	JAPANESE	ENGLISH
denki	電気	electric, lights
densha	電車	train
dentō	伝統	traditional
denwa	電話	telephone
depāto	デパート	department store
doa	ドア	door
dōbutsuen	動物園	zoo
doko	どこ	where
doku	毒	poison
dokusho	読書	reading
dore	どれ	which one
dōshite	どうして	why
Do-yōbi	土曜日	Saturday

E

e	絵	painting
eiga	映画	movie
eigakan	映画館	movie theater
Eigo	英語	English
Ejiputo	エジプト	Egypt
eki	駅	train station
ekitai	液体	liquid
en	円	yen
enpitsu	鉛筆	pencil
enpitsukezuri	鉛筆けずり	pencil sharpener
erebētā	エレベーター	elevator
esukarētā	エスカレーター	escalator

F

fōku	フォーク	fork
fugu	ふぐ	blowfish
fuhō	不法	illegal
fuku	服	clothes
fune	船	boat
Furansu	フランス	France
Furansugo	フランス語	French language
furonto	フロント	front desk
furui	古い	old (*vs. new*)

ROMAJI	JAPANESE	ENGLISH
futari	二人	two people
fūtō	封筒	envelope
futotteiru	太っている	is fat
futsū	普通	normal
fuyu	冬	winter

G

gaikoku	外国	foreign country
gaikokugo	外国語	foreign language
gaikoku-jin	外国人	foreigner
gakkō	学校	school
gakusei	学生	college student
gamu	ガム	gum
ganbarimasu	頑張ります	to do one's best
Ganbatte	頑張って	Good luck!
garēji	ガレージ	garage
gasorin	ガソリン	gasoline
gēmu	ゲーム	game
genkan	玄関	entrance, home
genki	元気	fine, healthy
genkin	現金	cash
geri	下痢	diarrhea
Getsu-yōbi	月曜日	Monday
gin	銀	silver
ginkō	銀行	bank
gochisōsama	ごちそうさま	phrase said after a meal
gogo	午後	p.m.
gohan	ご飯	rice (*cooked*)
gomi	ゴミ	garbage
gomibako	ゴミ箱	trashcan
gōru	ゴール	goal
gorufu	ゴルフ	golf
gōtō	強盗	robbery
gozen	午前	a.m.
gyūniku	牛肉	beef

ROMAJI	JAPANESE	ENGLISH

H

ha	歯	tooth
hābu	ハーブ	herb
hagaki	ハガキ	postcard
haikingu	ハイキング	hiking
haisha	歯医者	dentist
haitatsu suru	配達する	to deliver
hajimeru	始める	to start
hakike	吐き気	nausea
hamu	ハム	ham
hana	花	flower
hana	鼻	nose
hanabi	花火	fireworks
hanasu	話す	to speak
hanaya	花屋	florist
hanbāgā	ハンバーガー	hamburger
hankachi	ハンカチ	handkerchief
hantai suru	反対する	to disagree
harau	払う	to pay
hare	晴	sunny
haru	春	spring
hashi	橋	bridge
hashi	箸	chopsticks
hashigo	はしご	ladder
hashiru	走る	to run
hata	はた	flag
hayai	早い	quick
hayaku	早く	early, hurry
hayasa	速さ	speed
heijitsu	平日	weekday
heiwa	平和	peace
henji	返事	reply
heri	ヘリ	helicopter
heta	下手	not skillful
heya	部屋	room
hi	日	day
hi	火	fire
hidari	左	left (*direction*)

ROMAJI	JAPANESE	ENGLISH
hidoi	ひどい	is terrible
higashi	東	east
hiji	ひじ	elbow
hikōki	飛行機	airplane
hikui	低い	is short (*in height*)
hirune	昼寝	nap
hito	人	person
hitsuyō	必要	necessary
hiza	膝	knee
hoken	保険	insurance
hokkē	ホッケー	hockey
hon	本	book
hontō	本当	true, really
hon-ya	本屋	bookstore
hoshii	ほしい	want something
hoteru	ホテル	hotel
hottokēki	ホットケーキ	pancake

I

ichigo	いちご	strawberry
Igirisu	イギリス	Britain
ii	良い	good
iie	いいえ	no
ika	イカ	squid
ike	池	pond
iku	行く	to go
ikura	いくら	how much
ikutsu	いくつ	how many
ima	今	now
imasu	います	there is (*animate objects*)
imōto	妹	younger sister
Indo	インド	India
infuruenza	インフルエンザ	flu
inoru	祈る	to pray
Intānetto	インターネット	Internet
inu	犬	dog
ippai	いっぱい	full
iriguchi	入り口	entrance

ROMAJI	JAPANESE	ENGLISH
iro	色	color
isha	医者	doctor
isogashii	忙しい	busy
isogu	急ぐ	in a hurry
isu	いす	chair
Isuraeru	イスラエル	Israel
itadakimasu	いただきます	phrase said before a meal
itai	いたい	painful
itoko	いとこ	cousin
itsu	いつ	when
itsumo	いつも	always
izakaya	居酒屋	bar

J

jihan-ki	自販機	vending machine
jikan	時間	time
jimusho	事務所	office
jinkō	人口	population
jisaboke	時差ボケ	jet lag
jisho	辞書	dictionary
jitensha	自転車	bike
jiyū	自由	freedom
jagaimo	ジャガイモ	potato
jaketto	ジャケット	jacket
jama	じゃま	is a hindrance
jōdan	冗談	joke
josei	女性	female
jōzu	上手	skillful
jūdenki	じゅうでんき	charger
jugyō	授業	class
juku	塾	cram school
junban	順番	order (*sequence*)
jūsho	住所	address
jūsu	ジュース	juice

K

katsu	勝つ	to win
kafeteria	カフェテリア	cafeteria

ROMAJI	JAPANESE	ENGLISH
kaeru	かえる	frog
kagaku	科学	science
kagami	鏡	mirror
kagi	鍵	key
kai	階	floor
kaidan	階段	stairs
kau	買う	to buy
kaimono	買い物	shopping
kaisha	会社	company
kaishain	会社員	company employee
kaki	かき	oyster
kami	神	god
kami	髪	hair
kami	紙	paper
Kanada	カナダ	Canada
kanashii	悲しい	sad
kanemochi	金持ち	rich
kangoshi	看護師	nurse
kani	かに	crab
kanja	患者	patient (*sick person*)
Kankoku	韓国	Korea
Kankokugo	韓国語	Korean language
Kankoku-jin	韓国人	Korean citizen
kanō	可能	possible
kanojo	彼女	girlfriend
kanpeki	完ぺき	perfect
kansha	感謝	thankful
kao	顔	face
kaori	香り	aroma, fragrance
kara	空	empty
karada	体	body
kareshi	彼氏	boyfriend
kariru	借りる	to borrow
kasa	傘	umbrella
kata	かた	shoulder
katei	家庭	home
kawa	川	river
kawaii	かわいい	cute

ROMAJI	JAPANESE	ENGLISH
Kawaisō ni	かわいそうに	What a pity!
kawaita	乾いた	dry
Ka-yōbi	火曜日	Tuesday
kayumi	かゆみ	itch
kazan	火山	volcano
kaze	かぜ	a cold (*illness*)
kaze	風	wind
kazu	数	number
kechappu	ケチャップ	ketchup
keikaku	計画	plan
keikan	警官	police
keitai	携帯	mobile phone
keiyaku	契約	contract
keizai	経済	economy
kekkon suru	結婚する	to marry
ken	県	prefecture
kenkō	健康	health
keshigomu	消しゴム	eraser
ki	木	tree
kibishii	厳しい	strict
kiiro	きいろ	yellow
kiken	危険	danger
kiku	聞く	to listen
kikō	気候	climate
kimeru	決める	to decide
kin	金	gold
kinen	禁煙	nonsmoking
kinō	昨日	yesterday
Ka-yōbi	火曜日	Tuesday
Kin-yōbi	金曜日	Friday
kippu	切符	ticket
kirai	きらい	dislike
kirei	きれい	clean; pretty
kiri	きり	fog
Kirisuto-kyō	キリスト教	Christian
kiro	キロ	kilo
kisetsu	季節	season
kisoku	きそく	rule

ROMAJI	JAPANESE	ENGLISH
kissaten	喫茶店	coffee shop
kisu	キス	kiss
kita	北	north
kitanai	きたない	is dirty
kitte	切手	stamp
kōban	交番	police box
kochira	こちら	this one
kodomo	子供	child/children
koe	声	voice
kōen	公園	park
kōhii	コーヒー	coffee
kōjō	工場	factory
kōkan suru	交換	exchange
koko	ここ	here
kōkō	高校	high school
kokoro	心	spirit
kokunai	国内	domestic
kokuseki	国籍	nationality
kome	米	rice (*uncooked*)
konban	今晩	tonight
konbanwa	こんばんは	good evening
konbini	コンビニ	convenience store
konde iru	混んでいる	crowded
kongetsu	今月	this month
Kon'nichiwa.	こんにちは。	Good afternoon.
konsāto	コンサート	concert
kore	これ	this
kore kara	これから	from now on
kōri	氷	ice
koshō	こしょう	black pepper
kōto	コート	coat
kotoshi	今年	this year
kowai	こわい	scary
kozeni	小銭	coin
kuchi	口	mouth
kuchibiru	唇	lip
kūkō	空港	airport
kumo	雲	cloud

ROMAJI	JAPANESE	ENGLISH
kuni	国	country
kurai	くらい	dark
kurikaesu	繰り返す	to repeat
kuro	黒	black
kuruma	車	car
kusa	草	grass
kusuri	薬	medicine
kutsu	靴	shoes
kutsushita	靴下	sock
kyō	今日	today
kyōiku	教育	education
kyōkai	教会	church
kyonen	去年	last year
kyori	距離	distance
kyūjitsu	休日	holiday
kyūkyūsha	救急車	ambulance
kyūryō	給料	salary

M

ROMAJI	JAPANESE	ENGLISH
machigae	間違え	mistake
matsu	待つ	to wait
mada	まだ	yet
made	まで	until
mado	窓	window
mainen/maitoshi	毎年	every year
mainichi	毎日	every day
maishū	毎週	every week
makeru	負ける	to lose
man'naka	真ん中	middle
manshon	マンション	condominium
massugu	まっすぐ	straight ahead
mata	また	again
mayotte imasu	迷っています	(*I am*) lost
mazui	まずい	unappetizing
me	目	eye
megane	メガネ	glasses
meishi	名刺	namecard
men	めん	noodles

ROMAJI	JAPANESE	ENGLISH
menyū	メニュー	menu
menzeihin	免税品	duty-free item
michi	道	road
midori	緑	green
migi	右	right
mijikai	短い	is short (*not for height*)
mimi	耳	ear
mise	店	store
mizu	水	water
mizu'umi	湖	lake
mokuteki	目的	purpose
Moku-yōbi	木曜日	Thursday
mon	門	gate
mondai	問題	problem
mono	物	thing
monogatari	物語	story
motto	もっと	more
mura	村	village
murasaki	紫	purple
mushi	虫	insect
mushiatsui	むし暑い	hot and humid
musuko	息子	son
musume	娘	daughter
muzukashii	難しい	difficult

N

nabi	ナビ	GPS (*car navigation*)
naifu	ナイフ	knife
naka	中	inside
naku	泣く	to cry
nakushimasuhita	なくしました	lost it
nama	生	raw
namae	名前	name
nani	何	what
napukin	ナプキン	napkin
nashi	なし	pear
nasu	なす	eggplant
natsu	夏	summer

183

ROMAJI	JAPANESE	ENGLISH
naze	なぜ	why
nedan	値段	price
neko	猫	cat
nemui	眠い	sleepy
neru	寝る	to sleep
netsu	熱	fever
nezumi	ねずみ	mouse
Nichi-yōbi	日曜日	Sunday
Nihon	日本	Japan
Nihongo	日本語	Japanese language
Nihon-shoku	日本食	Japanese cuisine
niku	肉	meat
ninjin	にんじん	carrot
ninshin	妊娠	pregnant
nishi	西	west
ni wa	庭	garden
noboru	登る	to climb
nodo	のど	throat
nodo ga kawaita	のどがかわいた	thirsty
nomu	飲む	to drink
nomimono	飲み物	drinks
nori	のり	glue
nōto	ノート	notebook
nyūsu	ニュース	news

O

obasan	おばさん	aunt
obāsan	おばあさん	grandmother
ōbun	オーブン	oven
o-cha	お茶	green tea, tea
o-furō	お風呂	bath
o-hashi	お箸	chopsticks
o-hiru gohan	お昼ご飯	lunch
oisha-san	お医者さん	doctor
oishii	美味しい	delicious
ojisan	おじさん	uncle
ojiisan	おじいさん	grandfather
o-kaidokuhin	お買い得品	bargain

ROMAJI	JAPANESE	ENGLISH
okane	お金	money
o-kanjō	お勘定	restaurant check
okāsan	お母さん	mother
okawari	おかわり	second helping
okoru	怒る	to be angry
okureru	遅れる	to delay
o-kyaku	お客	customer
Omedetō gozaimasu!	おめでとうございます	Congratulations!
omiyage	お土産	souvenirs
o-mizu	お水	water
omocha	おもちゃ	toy
omoi	おもい	heavy
omoidasu	思い出す	to remember
o-musubi	おむすび	rice ball
onaji	同じ	same
onaka	おなか	stomach
onaka ga suita	おなかがすいた	hungry
onegai	お願い	favor
ongaku	音楽	music
on'na no ko	女の子	girl
ōi	おおい	many
ōkii	大きい	big
Oranda	オランダ	Netherlands
orenji	オレンジ	orange
o-shigoto	お仕事	job
o-shiro	お城	castle
osoi	遅い	late; slow
osu	押す	to push
Otanjōbi Omedetō	お誕生日おめでとう	Happy Birthday
o-tearai	お手洗い	bathroom
o-tenki	お天気	weather
oto	音	sound
otoko	男	male
otona	大人	adult
otōsan	お父さん	dad
ototoi	おととい	the day before yesterday
otsuri	おつり	change (*money returned*)
otto	夫	husband

ROMAJI	JAPANESE	ENGLISH
owari	終わり	end
oya	親	parent
oyogu	泳ぐ	to swim
o-yu	お湯	hot water

P

pajama	パジャマ	pajamas
pan	パン	bread
pasokon	パソコン	computer
pasupōto	パスポート	passport
pēji	ページ	page
pen	ペン	pen
penki	ペンキ	paint
pondo	ポンド	pound
Porutogaru	ポルトガル	Portugal

R

raigetsu	来月	next month
rainen	来年	next year
raishū	来週	next week
rei	れい	bow
reitōkō	冷凍庫	freezer
reizōkō	冷蔵庫	fridge
reji	レジ	cash register
rekishi	歴史	history
remon	レモン	lemon
renshū	練習	practice
ringo	りんご	apple
robii	ロビー	lobby
rokkā	ロッカー	locker
Roshia	ロシア	Russia
ryō	りょう	dorm
ryōhō	両方	both
ryōri no hon	料理の本	cookbook
ryōri suru	料理する	to cook
ryōshūsho	領収書	receipt

ROMAJI	JAPANESE	ENGLISH

S

sagasu	探す	to find
saigo	最後	final; last
saisho	最初	first
saizu	サイズ	size
sakana	魚	fish
sakkā	サッカー	soccer
sakura	さくら	cherry blossoms
samui	寒い	cold
sandoicchi	サンドイッチ	sandwich
sanso	酸素	oxygen
sara	皿	dish; plate
sayōnara	さようなら	goodbye (*with regret*)
seijika	政治家	politician
seiseki	成績	grades
seito	生徒	student
seki	せき	cough
seki	席	seat
sekken	石鹸	soap
senkyo	選挙	election
sensei	先生	teacher
senshū	先週	last week
sentaku	せんたく	laundry
senzai	洗剤	detergent
shakai	社会	social studies, society
shashin	写真	photo
shatsu	シャツ	shirt
shawā	シャワー	shower
shefu	シェフ	chef
shi	市	city
shi	詩	poem
shiawase	幸せ	happy
shiken	試験	exam
shimasu	します	to do
shimeru	閉める	to close
Shin'nen	新年	New Year
shinbun	新聞	newspaper
shinkansen	新幹線	bullet train

ROMAJI	JAPANESE	ENGLISH
shinsen	新鮮	fresh
shinu	死ぬ	to die
shinzō	心臓	heart
shio	塩	salt
shiro	白	white
shita	下	under
shitsurei	失礼	rude
shizen	自然	nature
shizuka	静か	quiet
shokudō	食堂	cafeteria
shokuji	食事	meal
shorui	書類	document
shōyu	醤油	soy sauce
shufu	主婦	home maker
shukuhaku	宿泊	accommodation
shūkyō	宗教	religion
shūnyū	収入	income
shuppatsu	出発	departure
shuppatsu suru	出発する	to depart
shūri	修理	repair
SNS	エスエヌエス	social media
sōjiki	掃除機	vacuum
sonkei	尊敬	respect
soko	そこ	there
soto	外	outside
sotsugyōshiki	卒業式	graduation
sūgaku	数学	math
Sui-yōbi	水曜日	Wednesday
suki	好き	like
sukii	スキー	ski
sumaho	スマホ	smartphone
suna	砂	sand
sūpā	スーパー	supermarket
suri	スリ	pickpocket
suru	する	to do
sushiya	寿司屋	sushi bar

ROMAJI	JAPANESE	ENGLISH

T

taberu	食べる	to eat
tabemono	食べ物	food
tada	ただ	free
tadashii	正しい	correct
Taiheiyō	太平洋	Pacific Ocean
taishikan	大使館	embassy
taishoku	退職	retire
takai	高い	expensive
takasa	高さ	height
taki	滝	waterfall
takusan	たくさん	many
takushii	タクシー	taxi
tamago	たまご	egg
tanoshii	楽しい	is fun
tasukete	助けて	help
tatemono	建物	building
tatsu	立つ	to stand
te	手	hand
tebukuro	手袋	glove
tegami	手紙	letter
te-nimotsu	手荷物	baggage
tenki	天気	weather
terebi	テレビ	television
tēshoku	定食	set menu
tōchaku	到着	arrival
tōi	遠い	far
toire	トイレ	toilet
tokei	時計	clock
tomodachi	友達	friend
tori	鳥	bird
toshokan	図書館	library
tsuā	ツアー	tour
tsudukeru	続ける	to continue
tsugi	次	next
tsukarete iru	疲れている	tired
tsukue	つくえ	desk
tsuri	釣り	fishing

ROMAJI	JAPANESE	ENGLISH
tsūro	通路	aisle
tsuyoi	強い	strong

U

uchi	うち	house
ude	うで	wrist
uma	馬	horse
umi	海	ocean, sea
unagi	うなぎ	eel
unchin	運賃	fare
undō	運動	exercise
unten suru	運転する	to drive
unten menkyoshō	運転免許証	driver's license
urikire	売り切れ	sold out
ureshii	嬉しい	is happy
urusai	うるさい	noisy
usagi	うさぎ	rabbit
ushiro	後ろ	rear
uso	うそ	a lie
uta	歌	song
utau	歌う	to sing
uwasa	うわさ	rumor

W

wakai	若い	young
warau	笑う	to laugh
waremono	割れ物	fragile
waribiki	割引	discount
warui	悪い	bad
wasuremono	忘れ物	lost item
watashi	私	I
watashi no	私の	mine

Y

yakusoku	やくそく	promise
yakyū	野球	baseball
yama	山	mountain
yameru	やめる	to quit

ROMAJI	JAPANESE	ENGLISH
yane	屋根	roof
yasai	野菜	vegetables
yasashii	優しい	is nice
yasui	安い	inexpensive
yomu	読む	to read
Yōroppa	ヨーロッパ	Europe
yoru	夜	night
yosan	予算	budget
yotei	予定	schedule
yoyaku suru	予約する	to reserve
yubi	ゆび	finger
yūbin	郵便	mail
yūbin bangō	郵便番号	postcode
yūbin kyoku	郵便局	post office
yūenchi	遊園地	amusement park
yūgata	夕方	evening
yuki	雪	snow
yume	夢	dream
yūmei	有名	famous

Z

zan'nen	残念	unfortunately
zasshi	ざっし	magazine
zenbu	全部	all
zenzen	全然	not at all
zettai ni	絶対に	absolutely
zubon	ズボン	pants, trousers
zutsū	頭痛	headache

ABOUT TUTTLE
"Books to Span the East and West"

Our core mission at Tuttle Publishing is to create books which bring people together one page at a time. Tuttle was founded in 1832 in the small New England town of Rutland, Vermont (USA). Our fundamental values remain as strong today as they were then—to publish best-in-class books informing the English-speaking world about the countries and peoples of Asia. The world has become a smaller place today and Asia's economic, cultural and political influence has expanded, yet the need for meaningful dialogue and information about this diverse region has never been greater. Since 1948, Tuttle has been a leader in publishing books on the cultures, arts, cuisines, languages and literatures of Asia. Our authors and photographers have won numerous awards and Tuttle has published thousands of books on subjects ranging from martial arts to paper crafts. We welcome you to explore the wealth of information available on Asia at **www. tuttlepublishing.com.**

Published by Tuttle Publishing, an imprint of Periplus Editions (HK) Ltd.

www.tuttlepublishing.com

Copyright © 2017 by Scott Rutherford
Cover images from Freepik.com. Interior images from Shutterstock.

Library of Congress Control Number: 2016955489

ISBN 978-4-8053-1862-1

Distributed by

North America, Latin America & Europe
Tuttle Publishing
364 Innovation Drive
North Clarendon,
VT 05759-9436, USA.
Tel: 1 (802) 773-8930
Fax: 1 (802) 773-6993
info@tuttlepublishing.com
www.tuttlepublishing.com

Japan
Tuttle Publishing
Yaekari Building, 3rd Floor
5-4-12 Osaki
Shinagawa-ku
Tokyo 141 0032
Tel: (81) 03 5437-0171
Fax: (81) 03 5437-0755
sales@tuttle.co.jp
www.tuttle.co.jp

Asia Pacific
Berkeley Books Pte. Ltd.
3 Kallang Sector #04-01
Kolam Ayer Industrial Park
Singapore 349278
Tel: (65) 6471-2178
Fax: (65) 6471-2179
inquiries@periplus.com.sg
www.periplus.com

28 27 26 25 24   10 9 8 7 6 5 4 3 2 1   2406VP   Printed in Malaysia

TUTTLE PUBLISHING® is a registered trademark of Tuttle Publishing, a division of Periplus Editions (HK) Ltd.